REAL MIRACLES

Indisputable Evidence That God Heals

H. Richard Casdorph, M.D., Ph.D.

Contact Information:
H. Richard Casdorph, M.D., Ph.D.
1703 Termino Ave., Ste. 201
Long Beach, CA 90804
Phone: 562-597-8716
Fax: 562-597-4616

All Scripture quotations are either from the *King James Version* of the Bible or the *Revised Standard Version*, © 1952 by Division of Christian Education of the National Council of the Churches of Christ in the United States of America.

Real Miracles
Copyright ©2003 by Bridge-Logos, ©1976 by Logos International **(The Miracles)**
All Rights Reserved
Printed in the United States of America
Library of Congress Catalog Card Number: 76-2330
International Standard Book Number: 0-88270-950X

Published by:
Bridge-Logos
P.O. Box 141630
Gainesville, FL 32614
www.bridgelogos.com

Editor: Neil Stringer
Cover Design: Andy Toman

Printed in the United States of America. All rights reserved.
Under International Copyright Law, no part of this publication may be reproduced. Stored, or transmitted by any means—electronic, mechanical, photographic (photocopy), recording, or otherwise—without written permission from the publishers.

To the memory of Kathryn Kuhlman

Table of Contents

Acknowledgments		9
Introduction		13
Chapter 1	Reticulum Cell Sarcoma of Right Pelvic Bone *Lisa Larios*	21
Chapter 2	Chronic Rheumatoid Arthritis with Severe Disability *Elfrieda Stauffer*	35
Chapter 3	Malignant Brain Tumor (Glioma) of the Left Temporal Lobe *Marie Rosenberger*	49
Chapter 4	Multiple Sclerosis *Marion Burgio*	63

The Miracles

Chapter 5	Arteriosclerotic Heart Disease *Marvin Bird*	83
Chapter 6	Carcinoma of the Kidney (Hypernephroma) With Diffuse Bony Metastases *B. Ray Jackson*	99
Chapter 7	Mixed Rheumatoid Arthritis and Osteoarthritis *Pearl Bryant, Ph.D.*	115
Chapter 8	Probable Brain Tumor vs. Infarction of the Brain *Anne Soults*	135
Chapter 9	Massive GI Hemorrhage with Shock, Instantly Healed *Paul Trousdale*	155
Chapter 10	Osteoporosis of the Entire Spine with Intractable Pain Requiring Bilateral Cordotomies *Delores Winder*	165
Chapter 11	A Physician's Conclusions	181
Appendix		191

Acknowledgments

The Holy Spirit made this book possible and directed its writing.

Miss Kathryn Kuhlman was most helpful in enabling me to investigate, evaluate and document hearings that have occurred through her ministry. She and Maggie Harmer supplied me with names, addresses and telephone numbers, and did not refuse me access to any information for which I had need. Nan Nagle typed and retyped the manuscript. I deeply appreciate her long hours of devotion. My thanks also to Jamie Beatty who joined us late in this work and yet made a significant contribution to its completion.

The people who are the subjects of this book also cooperated unselfishly, giving

The Miracles

freely of their time and effort to tell the truth about the magnificent power of God.

I wish to acknowledge with thanks the significant contribution of the following physicians who served as an impartial panel (without remuneration) to evaluate various aspects of the cases in this book which fell within their area of expertise. Where possible the data and information, x-rays, angiograms, etc. were presented as unknowns to the physicians for their candid opinions.

Dr. Richard Steiner, M.D., Diplomate of the American Board of Pathology and Head of the Department of Pathology at Long Beach Community Hospital, reviewed the slides on several of the patients confirming the diagnoses. He was also kind enough to provide us with the photomicrographs of tissue samples.

Dr. William Olson, M.D., Diplomate of the American Board of Internal Medicine, American Board of Nuclear Medicine, and Head of the Isotope Department at Long Beach Community Hospital reviewed a number of the scans and repeated the brain scan on one of the patients at no charge to the patient.

The following radiologists in the Department of Radiology at Long Beach Community Hospital gave opinions regarding a variety of x-rays, computer scans (EMI scan) and coronary angiograms on different patients described in this book. These physicians are all Diplomates of the American Board of Radiology. Their names are: D.R. Belville, M.D., W.F. Whipple, M.D., G.M. Duncan, M.D., J.A. Morgan, M.D., R.E. Chaney, M.D., Paul P. Lee, M.D.

Dr. Anselmo Pineda, M.D., Diplomate of the American Board of Neurosurgery was kind enough to review one of the chapters in the book and give an opinion regarding the accuracy of the information contained therein.

I wish also to acknowledge the cooperation of physicians across the country who have, at their own expense, mailed to me x-rays and resumes of the charts and records of the patients included in this book.

The names of the individuals discussed in this book have not been changed. These are real names of real people. The book talks about modern day miracles performed by a real God.

Introduction

The Sentence of Death

Did you ever wonder what it would be like to approach death? The people whose stories appear in this book have been seriously and critically ill. Most of them have been told by their physicians that they were going to die, or were so seriously ill that those around them expected them to die. Most of them had an almost instantaneous healing while attending a miracle service conducted by Kathryn Kuhlman.

Mrs. Rosenberger was healed at home after a night of prayer conducted by her husband and family in 1970 when she appeared to be near death due to a malignant brain tumor. Her recovery started without any medical treatment. Even her skeptical physicians have

The Miracles

called it a miracle. Mr. Paul Trousdale was instantly healed of massive gastrointestinal hemorrhaging when he had a vision in which Christ came and firmly grasped his left hand. He was flooded with a feeling of warmth and knew he was healed (and he was). This occurred in a hospital bed following prayer with his pastor.

I have documented these cases as accurately as possible, utilizing my professional and academic background. By checking the available medical records or consulting the patients' physicians, I sought to determine several things: that the individual had the disease he or she reported; that the diagnosis had been made by a competent medical authority; and that the reputed healing had been verified by physical examination and, where necessary, by laboratory studies. Each person studied in this book continues in vigorous health at the time of this writing. Only one of their hearings occurred less than a year prior to publication.

The fact that physicians told several of these people that they had a fatal or incurable disease should not cast doubt on those doctors' competence. On the contrary, it should certify the serious nature of the diseases and the dramatic nature of the hearings.

As a physician I attempted to document these stories as accurately and objectively as possible. However, I should acknowledge that I believe the miracles in the New Testament actually happened. I am a man of faith.

I personally believe that Jesus healed the sick, raised the dead and turned water into wine. And I believe these miracles can still occur today because Jesus said, "Truly, truly, I say to you, he who believes in me will also do the works that I do; and greater works than these will he do, because I go to the Father. Whatever you ask in my name I will do it, that the Father may be glorified in the Son; if you ask anything in my name I will do it" (John 14:12-14).

Most of the hearings depicted in this book have been associated with the ministry of Miss Kathryn Kuhlman. I have known her for over ten years and have intermittently attended her services at the Shrine Auditorium in Los Angeles. The ready availability of many people with well-documented claims to healing, some of which were even publicized in the news media, presented me with the unusual opportunity to compile them in a single book.

However, the healing of God is by no means limited to Kathryn Kuhlman or her services. Miss Kuhlman has said repeatedly that she is not a faith healer, that these hearings come from God, and that she is an instrument of His Holy Spirit. In fact many people are healed outside the Shrine, some have been healed at home after attending the service, and some are healed before the service starts, before Miss Kuhlman has made an appearance at all. And there are many other claims of divine healing from all over the world.

Why Are Some Not Healed?

The opposite side of the coin of healing is death or chronic disability. If some are healed why are others not? Healings are given by the mercy of God. St. Paul complained of a physical affliction, which he called a "thorn in the flesh." When he prayed about it he was told, "My grace is sufficient for you, for my power is made perfect in weakness" (2 Cor. 12:9). And Paul was not relieved of his thorn. Beyond that I should not venture to say more. The point of this book is not to find out why people become sick or why they are not all healed, but to learn if miracles of healing really occur.

The word miracle comes from the Latin *miraculum*, which came in turn from the verb *miror* meaning "to wonder at." When John the Baptist sent his disciples to ask Jesus if He were the Christ, Jesus told them to go back and tell John what they had heard and seen: the blind see, the deaf hear, lepers cleansed, and the dead raised up (see Matt.

11:2-6). John would have to decide for himself on the basis of the evidence.

In like manner we must decide if these people, who reported serious even critical illness, were indeed instantly transformed to vigorous health. They have given me permission to use their names and no false names are used anywhere in this book. Their physicians' names have, as a rule, been omitted.

The Mike Douglas Show

The first Wednesday in March 1975, I finally met with the radiologist who had serially reviewed the x-rays of Lisa Larios during her bout with cancer of the hip. It had taken me three months to get the appointment since he was the busy head of the Radiation Therapy department of a prominent Los Angeles Hospital. I reviewed the x-rays that had shown the lesion during its initial evaluation and also those taken after it disappeared when Lisa had visited the miracle service at the Shrine Auditorium on July 16, 1972. Miss Kuhlman had originally suggested that I look at her x-rays. Lisa was twelve years old when she had the tumor.

As I examined those pictures, I saw a malignant tumor of the hip socket, which had also invaded the soft tissues of the interior of the pelvis. A couple of days later I called Kathryn Kuhlman's Pittsburgh office

The Miracles

and left the message with Maryon Marsh that I had seen the films and was impressed because the lesion was much larger than I had expected from the description the Larios family physician had given me. I also told her the radiologist had been courteous enough to supply me with copies of the x-rays for my own research.

Maryon called back that afternoon and told me that Miss Kuhlman wanted to know if I would go on the Mike Douglas Show to discuss and perhaps present the case of Lisa Larios. Mike Douglas was planning to devote a segment of one of his shows to "faith healing" and had invited Miss Kuhlman to be present. She felt that she should not appear at that time and asked if I would. I said yes. Lisa, her mother, Mrs. Isabel Larios, and I flew from Los Angeles to Philadelphia on March 24th. The show had been scheduled for taping at the KYW-TV studios during the next day.

Early in the evening before the show, Mike's associate producer called to ask if he could meet with us to get acquainted. About seven o'clock we were settled around a table in one of the hotel dining rooms. He wanted to know every detail of Lisa's story. When I showed him the x-rays, he asked if there was some way he could verify that these were of Lisa and not someone else.

I was taken aback at first but I showed him the patient's name and age indelibly imprinted into the film, as well as the name of the hospital and the date on which the x-rays were taken. So far as I know there is no way to alter this standard imprinting. I gave him the name of the radiologist who supplied me with the copies of the x-rays, and his secretary's name, so that, if he wanted, he could call and ascertain that I had in fact visited with them and that they had supplied me with copies of Lisa's x-rays.

He seemed satisfied on that point and asked me if Miss Kuhlman had made financial contributions to my professional organization in Long Beach, California. He explained that he thought it wise to anticipate any question that skeptics in the audience might have. I told him I had not received any contributions from Miss Kuhlman. Nor, I explained, had Miss Kuhlman paid my expenses for the research on this book.

I gave the associate producer a copy of my curriculum vitae, a succinct survey of my personal and professional background. It is included as an appendix to this book.

With the questions over we freshened up a bit and returned to the same restaurant for a late dinner. Our rooms at the hotel were on the sixteenth floor. Earlier we had done some shopping in the lobby and were about to

The Miracles

return to our rooms. Lisa decided she wanted to climb the stairs, and she did, all the way to the sixteenth floor. It was a wonderful demonstration of her vigorous health. After dinner and a brief walk we turned in. The next day we would tell Lisa's story to the nation via the Mike Douglas Show.

Chapter 1

Reticulum Cell Sarcoma of Right Pelvic Bone

Lisa Larios

LISA LARIOS IS A BRIGHT, ATTRACTIVE, bouncy teenager. On the trip to Philadelphia she played tricks on her mother, giggled and generally had a good time.

Up to the time she developed right hip pain in 1972, Lisa considers that she had had a normal life. She was named Elizabeth Valenzuela at birth, but her parents divorced each other when she was five. When her mother remarried she took her stepfather's name, Larios.

She and her mother were nominal Catholics prior to her healing at the Shrine Auditorium. They attended mass only three

The Miracles

or four times a year. However, when she was ten Lisa awakened out of sleep one night and had a vision of the Virgin Mary in her bedroom. The Virgin was totally red. I asked her how she knew it was the Virgin and she said, "Well, I just knew because of the way she was dressed." All the features were clearly identifiable, except the face, which was not well seen, but she had no doubt that she had seen a vision of the Virgin. In spite of this she did not consider herself to be an overly religious individual and did not remember dreaming at night, except perhaps on rare occasions, prior to her healing.

In March of 1972 Lisa gradually developed pain, which she described as a burning or pulling sensation in the right hip. Associated with this was a limp because of pain on weight-bearing. In May she was hospitalized by her family physician and an appendectomy was performed. Her appendix was acutely inflamed and they thought this might have accounted for the hip pain.

However, in the post-operative period the pain recurred in the same area. X-rays revealed a lesion of the right hip socket. On May 15, 1962, she entered St. Joseph's Hospital in Burbank and, ten days later, was taken to surgery for exploration and biopsy of the right pelvic bone by her family physician and an orthopedic surgeon. The malignancy involved the right ileum and the doctors thought at first that it was Ewing's sarcoma. However, after several pathologists examined the biopsy slides, they changed their diagnosis to reticulum cell sarcoma of bone.

For three weeks prior to that surgery, Lisa had been unable to bear weight on the right lower extremity because of the pain. She had to get about on crutches or in a wheelchair. She would not walk on her right leg again until the day of her healing at the Shrine Auditorium.

In the first week of June she went to the Los Angeles Children's Hospital. Physicians there reviewed the slides and confirmed the diagnosis. The slides were sent to other institutions for confirmation. This is the policy at L.A. Children's Hospital before beginning cancer chemotherapy. She was under the care of the head of chemotherapy, a hematologist, and the head of the radiation therapy department. They authorized many diagnostic studies, including kidney x-rays, x-rays of the involved bones, bone marrow aspiration, etc. From these they learned that the tumor had extended from the pelvic bone into the pelvis, approximately seven centimeters (2.58 inches) into the soft tissues. The tumor was palpable also upon rectal examination.

Once they had confirmed the diagnosis,

The Miracles

the doctors advised the use of radiation therapy to the hip plus cancer chemotherapy. They explained potential risks of both kinds of therapy to the mother and family, and there was considerable concern about whether Lisa should be subjected to the risks of chemotherapy.

Mrs. Larios thought the physicians said that without therapy Lisa could be expected to live about six months, but with the radiation and chemical therapy she might live longer. With that in mind she consented to the use of chemotherapy and a series of injections were planned. However, Lisa received only the first injection. The following day the family decided not to allow her to have any additional therapy. Lisa had vomited repeatedly after that first injection and Mrs. Larios' alarm was heightened when her family priest told them about a family member of his who had undergone cancer chemotherapy. After weighing the pros and cons the family decided that Lisa would not have any radiation therapy at all nor any additional injections.

I talked with the hematologist who had superintended Lisa's abbreviated chemotherapy. She said that they felt very strongly at the time that Mrs. Larios had made the wrong decision in not allowing them to continue therapy. She would not tell me the exact dosage administered to Lisa in the one injection, but said that this was only part of the anticipated therapy and would not have had any significant effect on the tumor.

Lisa's condition remained essentially the same. She had lost about fifteen pounds during the course of her illness and still required pain medication. She was still unable to bear weight on the right lower extremity and had been advised not to because of the weakened condition of the bone socket.

Figures 1 and 2 show the x-rays taken in June 1972. In them we can see the extensive nature of the bone tumor and evidence of its spread into the soft tissues of the pelvis. Inasmuch as this extensive tumor involves the bone socket, it is apparent why any weight-bearing on this extremity might cause pain.

A close friend of the family by the name of Bill Truit kept encouraging Mrs. Larios to bring Lisa to one of the healing services of Kathryn Kuhlman at the Shrine Auditorium. He told her he believed Lisa was going to get well. Mrs. Larios finally agreed to attend on July 16, 1972. Lisa went only to please her mother who told her she wanted to get out of the house.

Lisa did not know that her bony tumor was malignant. She thought it had been removed at the time of surgery (the biopsy)

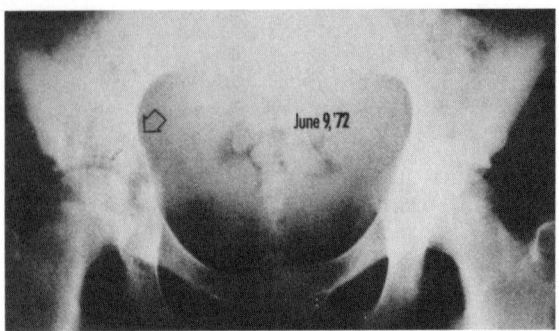

Figure 1: *X-ray of Lisa Larios' pelvic bone taken from the front, June 9, 1972, showing extensive destruction of the right hip joint (the acetabulum). Compare this with the normal whitish density of the left hip socket.*

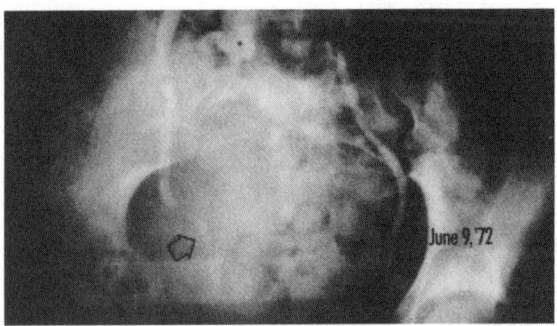

Figure 2: *Kidney x-ray (intravenous pyelogram) of Lisa taken from the front, June 9, 1972. The arrow points to the right ureter which shows up as a whitish line. Note that it is being pushed away from the hip by the tumor which has invaded this part of the pelvis from its base in the hip bone. Again the darkened areas of the right hip bone show destruction, while the left hip bone appears normally white.*

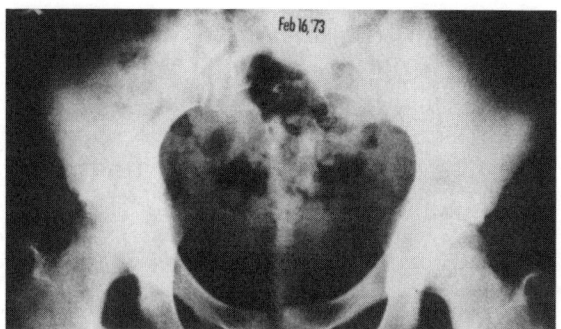

Figure 3: *Routine follow-up x-ray of Lisa's pelvis taken February 16, 1973. The two hip bones appear equally normally at this time. Compare with figure 1. See text for discussion.*

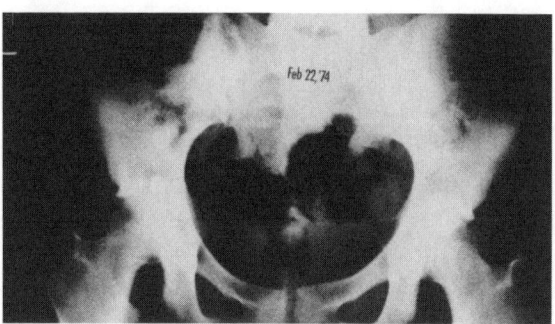

Figure 4: *Routine follow-up x-ray of Lisa's pelvis taken February 22, 1974. The pelvis is radiographically within normal limits. Compare with figure 1. See text discussion.*

The Miracles

from which she was still convalescing and, because of this, she had hip pain and still needed to walk on crutches. She suspected nothing. During the week prior to their visit to the Shrine Auditorium, Bill Truit fasted and drank only water. Finally the day came and they made the trip to the Shrine Auditorium. Lisa sat in the wheelchair section with her mother.

During the service Lisa complained to her mother of a warm sensation in her stomach. But, when Isabel Larios suggested she might want something to eat, Lisa said, "No, I'm not hungry, I have a warm feeling" and she pointed to the pit of her stomach.

About this time Miss Kuhlman pointed and said, "Someone in the wheelchair section is getting a healing for cancer. Stand up and take your healing."

Remember, Lisa did not know that she had cancer, but she turned to her mother and said, "Can I stand up? I think I can walk now." Her mother was skeptical, "No, sit down."

An usher came along about then and asked what was going on. Lisa said, "I feel like I want to get up and walk around. I can't explain it, I just suddenly have the urge to get up and walk." When Mrs. Larios explained the situation to the usher, he said, "Well, this is a miracle service and these things sometimes happen."

After the discussion, Mrs. Larios allowed Lisa to get up and walk. She was completely free of pain. This is the first time Lisa Larios had walked since three weeks prior to her surgery, and the first time that she had been totally free of pain. She walked and then ran and went up on the stage to tell of her healing. Bill Truit went with her and only then, when he told Miss Kuhlman about the cancer of the hip, did Lisa learn the true nature of her hip lesion.

Up on the stage Lisa walked, ran and did exercises completely free of pain, and has remained free of pain to this date. When Miss Kuhlman prayed for her, Lisa fell on the floor. I asked her what it felt like and she said you lose consciousness for a minute or two. Her mother had a similar experience when Miss Kuhlman prayed for her.

When they returned home that day, Lisa promptly went out bicycle riding. In the days that followed she rapidly regained the weight she had lost. She has been running and playing ever since and leads a completely normal life.

Not long after that, Mrs. Larios brought Lisa back to Children's Hospital for some previously scheduled x-rays of the pelvis. Mrs. Larios was still uncertain that a real healing had occurred and she was eager to learn the results of this appointment. The x-rays were other doctors about the unexpected finding on the x-rays. She said called her back by Friday afternoon, Mrs. Larios called her because she did not want to wait over the weekend. The doctor said that she had been delayed because she had consulted with several other doctors about the unexpected findings on the x-rays. She said there was definite improvement and signs of healing. At this point Mrs. Larios allowed herself to believe that her daughter would possibly be well again.

They took x-rays of Lisa's hip about every six weeks after that, and they all showed continued improvement. The x-ray of February 16, 1973, showed almost complete resolution (Figure 3). Only a skilled reader could pick up minor variation in the bony architecture evident on this film. The film taken in February 1974 shows a completely normal hip (Figure 4).

On November 7, 1974, Lisa had some sort of seizure while at home. An ambulance rushed to the home to take her to the hospital. She had turned blue and, after arriving at the hospital, had a period of amnesia for the immediate events, but this cleared shortly. The family doctor was happy to have her in the hospital so that he could check her over completely. He ordered complete studies including upper and lower GI x-rays, chest x-ray, hip x-rays, and a brain scan. All were normal, except focal dysrhythmia on an electroencephalogram. The family doctor concluded that there was no evidence of recurrence of the tumor.

Summary and Comment

We have been able to document the pertinent features of this very interesting story and have some medical records from each of the hospitals involved.

She was initially admitted to St. Joseph's Hospital in Burbank where the biopsy of the tumor was obtained. The doctors initially thought that this was a Ewing's sarcoma of the right innominate bone. But, after several pathologists reviewed the slide, they concluded that the patient had a different type of tumor, reticulum cell sarcoma of bone.

Richard Steiner, M.D., Head of the Department of Pathology at Long Beach Community Hospital reviewed the slides and he concurs with the final diagnosis.

Medical treatment was certainly minimal inasmuch as the patient received no radiation therapy and only one injection of medication that the hematologist in charge did not think would have a significant effect on the tumor.

Two factors point away from the idea that Lisa's rapid improvement might be due to the power of suggestion. On careful questioning she states that the warm feeling in her stomach started first and, after that, Miss Kuhlman pointed in her direction and said, "Someone is getting a healing for cancer." Miss Kuhlman repeated, "Someone is getting a healing for cancer in the wheelchair section. Stand up and take your healing." Lisa still did not know that she had cancer and it seems unlikely that she would have responded to a suggestion that seemed inappropriate to her own circumstances.

Not only has the patient been healed physically, but there has been considerable spiritual change as well. Lisa told me she didn't pray or meditate much prior to her healing, but now she prays to God daily for others. Her dream life has changed. She does not recall dreaming at all prior to her healing, but now she dreams nightly in color and, in some of her dreams, she has talked to the Virgin Mary.

Figure 5: Mr. & Mrs. Stauffer after her healing from rheumatoid arthritis.

Chapter 2

Chronic Rheumatoid Arthritis with Severe Disability

Elfrieda Stauffer

ELFRIEDA STAUFFER WAS THE FIRST CASE I researched and I thought for a while it might be my last. In November 1974, Miss Kuhlman came to town for her monthly service at the Shrine Auditorium, and I talked to Miss Maggie Hartner and her about authenticating and documenting some of the hearings that had occurred through her ministry. Miss Kuhlman liked the idea and suggested I start with the case of Elfrieda Stauffer who lived near San Diego. They said Mrs. Stauffer had had rheumatoid arthritis and gave me her address and telephone number.

The Miracles

I called Mrs. Stauffer shortly after that and later met both her and her husband in Los Angeles. Within a week or two I had obtained a copy of her medical records from the Scripp's Clinic whose rheumatologist she had seen in consultation. These records confirmed a diagnosis of chronic rheumatoid arthritis. The following month at the service at the Shrine Auditorium, Miss Kuhlman called both Mrs. Stauffer and myself up to the stage where I told Elfrieda's story and said I had confirmed that a diagnosis had been made by a competent medical authority and that she was now well.

After the service Maggie Hartner said she had appreciated my testimony and asked if I would appear with Mrs. Stauffer on Miss Kuhlman's television show. I said yes. But later I began to have misgivings. During the nine months prior to Elfrieda's healing, when her condition was most severe, approaching critical proportion, she had been under treatment by a physician in Mexico and I couldn't get medical records from him. This was the only case that I had documented at that time and I felt uneasy about the conclusions I could draw from it. As the telecast drew nearer, I became quite troubled about the matter and finally, the Saturday before the telecast, I called Miss Kuhlman's Pittsburgh office to say I thought it would be preferable to delay the telecast until I obtained more records. By this time all the arrangements had been made for the telecast, including hotel accommodations for the Stauffers who were to drive up from San Diego. I thought that Miss Kuhlman and the Stauffers might be offended by my decision, though I felt strangely relieved after having made it. I thought my action might make Miss Kuhlman decide not to want me to investigate any other cases. However, this was not so. She was very gracious about the matter and so were the Stauffers.

What is Rheumatoid Arthritis?

According to Cecil and Loeb's *A Textbook of Medicine*, rheumatoid arthritis is a systemic disease marked by inflammatory changes throughout the connective tissue of the body. It characteristically involves joints with a predilection for smaller joints, such as those of the hands and feet (technically called the proximal interphalangeal, the metacarpophalangeal and the metatarsophalangeal joints). The inflammation tends to distribute symmetrically after the disease has become established. The chronic proliferative inflammation of the synovial membrane that produces the arthritis can irreversibly damage the joint capsule and articular cartilage, which are replaced by granulation tissue.

The Miracles

Diagnosis: Although the diagnosis of a typical case of rheumatoid arthritis is usually obvious, recognition of an early case may be more difficult. Important features of the diagnosis are:

1. The tendency to occur in young adults although it may occur at any age.
2. The migratory character of the joint symptoms, particularly in the early stages.
3. The affected joints are usually swollen and tender.
4. Rheumatoid arthritis typically involves certain characteristic joints of the fingers and often results in fusiform fingers.
5. In severe cases the disease may eventually lead to deformity or ankylosis of the joint.
6. Laboratory findings are helpful, the high sedimentation rate is important, x-ray findings which are not absolutely specific are quite characteristic, if present. The positive agglutination or other seralogic tests are valuable if positive, but a negative test does not exclude the diagnosis.

Cecil and Loeb,
A Textbook of Medicine

The rheumatoid factor, sometimes found in the blood and detected by certain agglutination techniques, is present much less frequently in juvenile rheumatoid arthritis (10-20%), than in adult rheumatoid arthritis (65-85%).

What Is a Spontaneous Remission?

Rheumatoid arthritis is one of the diseases in which remissions may gradually occur. Unexplained improvement in any disease is known as spontaneous remission. If a patient improves as a result of drug therapy we say the disease goes into remission. Spontaneous or not, remission is invariably a gradual process, typically occurring over a period of days, weeks or months.

The day Elfrieda Stauffer was brought to the Shrine Auditorium she was critically ill. She could not dress herself or even walk to the bathroom unaided. During the service she emerged from this severe disability to complete normalcy within a matter of seconds or minutes. That is not spontaneous remission.

The Story of Elfrieda Stauffer

Elfrieda had joint pains in childhood, and she remembers her mother taping her wrists for support. Somersaults on the lawn with other children would send her into the house crying because of the pain in her wrists. Her wrists were often taped for days to relieve the pain. Joint pains came and went throughout her life as she grew to adulthood. The chief rheumatologist at the Scripp's Clinic confirmed that she must have been born with this form of arthritis.

In 1956 she had surgery on both feet in an attempt to relieve the pain that had developed in them by that time. Unfortunately the attempt failed and the discomfort gradually worsened. She saw the rheumatologist on July 8, 1971, and he diagnosed chronic rheumatoid arthritis, anatomic class 11, functional class 1. Foot x-rays revealed some early erosions, and perhaps an early cystic change.

Following this, she returned to the care of her regular internist who is a Fellow of the American College of Physicians. He prescribed a variety of drugs that are traditionally used to treat chronic rheumatoid arthritis, including Indocin, Butazolidin, and injections of gold salts. But each drug seemed to have some kind of side effect, which made it intolerable to the patient. Finally her internist told her there was nothing more he could do for her.

Elfrieda had heard of a doctor across the border in Mexicali who was having some success treating arthritis. She went to see him. He prescribed some pills and told her to take one a day. Within two days she had complete relief and was exhilarated. She went to Hawaii with her husband and, the following July, to Germany. She was back home just four days when, all of a sudden, the pain recurred. She returned to see her physician in Mexicali who treated her with one medication after another without further success. In September she spent two weeks in the Mexicali hospital after she had become quite ill while on another trip.

At this time many people in her church were praying for her. In particular her husband, Cliff, stood by her, praying for her, spending many nights literally on his knees. He kept reassuring her that God would heal her. Elfrieda was in severe pain throughout her body, but she also maintained her faith in God, thankful for her early training. When she was a child her father gave her twenty-five cents to learn the ninety-first Psalm. It was quite long, and she was the first one of her brothers and sisters to learn it.

> *He that dwelleth in the secret place of the most High shall abide under the shadow of the Almighty.*
> *I will say of the Lord, He is my refuge and my fortress: my God; in him will I trust.*
> *Surely he shall deliver thee from the snare of the fowler, and from the noisome pestilence.*

The Miracles

He shall cover thee with his feathers, and under his wings shalt thou trust: his truth shall be thy shield and buckler.

Thou shalt not be afraid for the terror by night; nor for the arrow that flieth by day;

Nor for the pestilence that walketh in darkness; nor for the destruction that wasteth at noonday.

A thousand shall fall at thy side, and ten thousand at thy right hand; but it shall not come nigh thee.

Only with thine eyes shalt thou behold and see the reward of the wicked.

Because thou hast made the Lord, which is my refuge, even the most High, thy habitation;

There shall no evil befall thee, neither shall any plague come nigh thy dwelling.

For he shall give his angels charge over thee, to keep thee in all thy ways.

They shall bear thee up in their hands, lest thou dash thy foot against a stone.

Thou shalt tread upon the lion and adder: the young lion and the dragon shalt thou trample under feet.

Because he hath set his love upon me, therefore will I deliver him: I will set him on high, because he hath known my name.

*He shall call upon me, and I will answer
him: I will be with him in trouble; I will
deliver him, and honour him.
With long life will I satisfy him, and shew
him my salvation.* (Psalm 91)

Many hours during the night, while Cliff was asleep, she would just lie in bed and repeat the ninety-first Psalm along with the even more familiar twenty-third Psalm.

Elfrieda told me that in a real trial it pays to have memorized some Scriptures, such as the above Psalm. She said she was grateful that she had learned the Scriptures, and learned to depend on them, especially since she could not even hold a book in her hand because of pain and swelling. Another of her favorites is a verse from the thirty-seventh Psalm: "Take delight in the Lord, and he will give you the desires of your heart. " Elfrieda believed that Jesus Christ is the same yesterday, today and forever. She believed that God could heal her, but she wanted Him to heal her right there in her bed.

Friends had urged her to attend a Kathryn Kuhlman meeting at the Shrine Auditorium, but Elfrieda did not believe in that kind of thing. Her father, however, ushered at the Kathryn Kuhlman meeting in Los Angeles for five years and came down each month to tell her about all the wonderful hearings. But

The Miracles

Elfrieda remained immovable in her belief that it wasn't necessary to go to a special healing service.

Finally a girl friend persuaded her to go to a Kathryn Kuhlman service, but just before she planned to go she became violently ill and could not attend. They tried again the next month, and once more she became quite ill. Her face was markedly swollen and the joints throughout her body hurt. She was unable to dress herself unaided and her hands were so swollen in the morning that she couldn't open them. But this time she decided that she would go to the next service even if they had to carry her on a stretcher.

Finally she did make it to the Shrine Auditorium on January 14, 1974. During the service Miss Kuhlman announced to all the people who had come with pain in the shoulders and feet, "You've been healed, just step into the aisle." Her words were calm and she said nothing more. Elfrieda looked around and thought, "How in the world do people know that they've been healed so fast?" She was very skeptical. Not only were her shoulders sore, but every joint and muscle in her body gave her extreme pain. At 2:50 she felt her left wrist and there was no pain, then her left forearm, still no pain. Next she tried to raise that arm and it went all the way up. When she checked her other wrist and found absolutely no pain, she tried to raise her right arm and it went up all the way. She began to get excited.

Then she started feeling the muscles in her legs. How many times had she tried to take a step and fallen to the floor, there to wait until someone picked her up and put her back in bed? But now there was no pain in her legs. "Well," she thought, "if I can wiggle my toes and my feet do not hurt, that will be it." They wiggled painlessly! This was the most exciting experience of her lifetime.

Again she wiggled her toes and stood up without assistance. A lady came to her, "Do you think you have been healed?"

"Yes, from rheumatoid arthritis, this is a miracle, I feel great! All the little things that people do, like housework, shampooing one's own hair, reading a book, were hers again - things that she had been deprived of for so many years.

She was escorted to the platform; it was exciting for her just to walk up the ramp that led to it. On stage Jimmy McDonald, Miss Kuhlman's soloist, began to lead Elfrieda toward a long line of people. But Miss Kuhlman saw them and called them over. At the microphone Miss Kuhlman had her lift up her knees and do all sorts of things she formerly could not have done.

Then she asked Elfrieda's husband, father

The Miracles

and mother to come to the stage and urged the whole congregation to stand and praise God for this healing. Thereupon, two generations of Elfrieda's family found themselves flat on their backs; not because Miss Kuhlman had prayed for and laid hands on them, but because of their proximity to her during this time of heightened worship. Elfrieda said that just before she fell down she saw a distinct halo about Miss Kuhlman's head.

After the service, at dinner, Cliff realized the swelling of her face was rapidly subsiding, and for the first time in a long time he could see a dimple in her cheek.

A week later she went on a Caribbean cruise and participated in all the normal activities. She has continued well and active and has not taken any of her former medicines, except for aspirin tablets for an occasional headache.

Today, Elfrieda thinks that God somehow wanted her to be healed in a religious service to obviate speculation that she went into spontaneous remission or that the drugs which she was taking had gradually had this effect.

Since her healing, Elfrieda has begun talking to various religious groups and churches, and has appeared on several television shows.

Comment

This case is well documented. I have copies of the consultation of the rheumatologist at the Scripp's Clinic and letters from her internist in San Diego. The patient was clearly incapacitated until shortly before three o'clock on the afternoon of January 14, 1974, when, in a matter of seconds or minutes, she was instantly restored to full vigorous health -free of pain - by the power of God!

Figure 6: *Rev. & Mrs. H.D. Rosenberger after her healing from a brain tumor.*

Chapter 3

Malignant Brain Tumor (Glioma of the Left Temporal Lobe)

Mrs. Marie Rosenberger

SOMETIME IN MARCH 1970, WHEN MRS. Marie Rosenberger was forty-four, she developed what she calls a "drastic" headache, diarrhea and weight loss. She was admitted to Hollywood Community Hospital in early May and underwent extensive studies. She had surgery on May 4th, where a neurosurgeon performed a left temporal craniectomy and partial resection of the tumor. The pathologist confirmed that it was a malignant astrocytoma, grade I. Dr. Richard Steiner, the head pathologist at Long Beach Community Hospital, reviewed the slides and confirmed the diagnosis of an astrocytoma or glioma, except that he assigned it grade II. Physicians explained to Mrs. Rosenberger's family that a tumor (about the size of a golf ball) had been removed but they had not been able to get all of it.

Mrs. Rosenberger left the hospital the next week, and began cobalt teletherapy on May 13th. The therapy was, of course, applied to the left temporal lobe of the brain for the malignant astrocytoma. On July 27th, after a three-week rest, additional treatment was given to the left temporal lobe, lateral, anterior and posterior fields. The total tissue dose to the lobe was 6,220 roentgens (6,005 rads).

Unfortunately, after the cessation of the cobalt treatments, her course was generally downhill. She temporarily had some command of her speech but gradually this diminished and she developed aphasia. She was unable to read, write or speak and the gradual downhill course continued for about a year until she was hospitalized in August 1971. She underwent a second carotid angiogram (see figure 8) and the neurosurgeon told them that the tumor was growing back. He advised additional surgery or chemotherapy, and asked the family to decide between them. However, Herman Rosenberger thought of a third option, the possibility of divine healing. He was, after all,

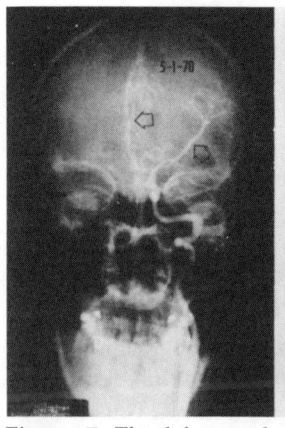
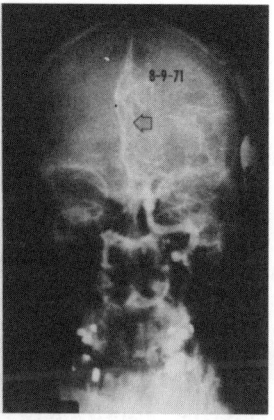

Figure 7: *This left carotid arteriogram of Marie Rosenberger taken May 1, 1970, reveals a deviation of her anterior cerebral artery across the midline to the right side (see upper arrow). The significant elevation and medial displacement of the left middle cerebral artery indicates a mass lesion below this point in the region of the left temporal lobe.*

Figure 8: *On August 9th, clinicians performed a second left carotid arteriogram on Marie. Again there was a shift of the anterior cerebral artery from the left to the right across the midline. Findings were consistent with residual or recurrent mass in the left temporal region.*

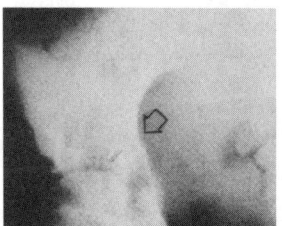

Figure 9: *This is the way Mrs. Rosenberger's brain tumor (glioma) tissue appeared when viewed under a microscope.*

an ordained minister with the Four Square Church and Dean of Students of the LIFE Bible College.

He talked it over with the family and decided to discontinue medical therapy and rely entirely on the healing ministry of the Holy Spirit for Marie. This decision was to have far-reaching effects on the lives of the people involved, especially Reverend Rosenberger's. He had no regrets about his wife's hospitalization and excellent medical care. He simply felt led to rely on the Holy Spirit for divine healing.

Herman brought his wife home and set himself to prayer. He also asked for prayer from the Angelus Temple Prayer Tower, Oral Roberts University Prayer Tower, and Miss Kuhlman's Pittsburgh office. The churches in which Reverend Rosenberger had been a pastor also joined in. All of this prayer culminated in the Rosenberger home after a Sunday evening church service that same August. Herman called his family together for a night of prayer in the kitchen.

They began about ten-thirty, but within two hours, only Marie's mother and Herman remained in the kitchen. About midnight Herman went out to rest on the couch. At two o'clock he came back and began, by the Holy Spirit, to pray in a manner that was beyond his own capabilities. He prayed for a solid hour with groaning and travail in English and in other tongues. All the Scriptures that he had ever memorized on divine healing came to his mind. At the end of that hour he was sure that Marie would be well. The assurance came as the Holy Spirit relieved the deep agony of prayer and said to him that his wife would be well from the top of her head to the soles of her feet. God specifically promised to restore her speech and vision. In fact Herman even had a vision of the tumor breaking up and being destroyed. Excitedly, Herman told the others who were beginning to awaken by then. They agree, in retrospect, that the miracle actually took place that Monday morning at three o'clock.

The next day they saw only slight improvement in Marie. But things really began to happen that evening. The family had re-gathered for prayer in the living room with Marie present and, although they did not see Him visually, they felt sure the Lord Jesus Himself was standing amongst them. They had concluded their devotions and the feeling persisted strongly. Herman spoke to the Lord, honoring His presence in the living room. The Lord replied in the silent voice of the Spirit that Marie soon would no longer need medication. Herman turned to Marie, "If I could see inside of your cranium right

The Miracles

now what would be going on?" As soon as the words were out he felt foolish.

"Oh! There's a popping and a crackling! My ear just opened!" Marie exclaimed. "Well, in Jesus' name, the tumor is gone." Again he felt foolish, but the Holy Spirit encouraged him to go on talking. "One of these mornings, Marie, you will not need medication."

The next morning she stopped taking it, and has not taken any since then. The medication was Dilantin to control eye and mandibular (lower jaw bone) seizures (secondary to the tumor). Once she stopped using the Dilantin, the seizures gradually subsided. In a matter of days there were no seizures, and they have not recurred. She continued to improve gradually, according to the original prophecy that Herman had received. Her speech was restored and then her vision.

They went back to see the neurosurgeon about a month after that. He found that she was markedly improved and asked what medication she had been taking. He had originally phoned in a prescription for chemotherapy to the drug store, but Marie had never taken it. Herman was cautious, not wanting to affront the doctor.

"If you have not been taking medicine, what have you done?"

"We've prayed."

"What else have you done or taken?"

"Nothing."

The neurosurgeon examined her again and found no signs of increased intercranial pressure. "I don't know what to tell you except keep on doing whatever you are doing."

They returned six months later and the neurosurgeon examined her again. "I just don't know what to tell you. This is obviously an answer to your prayers. This is remarkable. I want to see her again.

Herman and Marie prayed each time, before they went to see him, that the doctor would say something about this, miracle to glorify God.

At the time of our interview, Marie was not holding down an outside job. She was working at home and enjoying it, doing laundry and housework, playing the piano and doing her needle punch work. After her recovery she and her husband went to the Y.M.C.A. to swim regularly. They bought bicycles and rode together frequently. They also walked two miles each day and often went to the driving range. They spent two recent summer vacations in Sequoia National Forest, roughing it, camping out, and catching trout for breakfast. She travels east with her husband at Christmas time, and goes with him everywhere on his speaking engagements. She is very active in social work - she is a spunky gal!

The Miracles

At that same interview, Herman offered an intriguing interpretation of his experience leading up to that memorable night of prayer when God assured him that Marie would be healed. He explained to me that, after he brought her home from the hospital, Marie's condition was very bad. He and the rest of the family felt they were losing the battle for her life. At 101 pounds she was a shadow of her former self.

Herman confessed, "I had lost faith. I had virtually nothing in me but a sense of emptiness. By myself I was incapable of the kind of faith I knew was needed for a healing of this sort.

"God alone could bestow it on me as a gift of the Spirit. The Bible mentions healing, miracles, and faith as gifts in I Corinthians 12. They form a trinity, which seems to work in a special way. I see now that God was waiting until I was aware of my utter lack.

"Then I learned the difference between human faith, which is as good as nothing, and God's faith. His faith fell on me like a mantle and swept aside every fear and doubt. God poured it on me when I let my own go. And it came with an overwhelming sense of the Lord's presence, which stayed with us for months after that. The power of His presence emboldened us to fear nothing. If Marie took a turn for the worse, we didn't quake with fear. We would rebuke the illness in the name of Jesus and command it to depart! It never failed to obey either."

There is an epilogue, especially exciting to me, to the story of Marie Rosenberger. It came from a casual remark I made during our interview. Marie, in spite of her healing, spoke somewhat haltingly and sometimes mixed up her words.

Her problem was not hard to understand. The tumor had involved the dominant hemisphere of her brain and produced expressive aphasia as noted before. And, as is almost inevitable in the kind of surgery she underwent, the neurosurgeon had removed some of the dominant temporal lobe of her brain in an effort to try to rid her of as much of the malignancy as possible. I told Herman this and said I didn't think it detracted from her healing at all.

Then I unconsciously changed the subject and told him I thought Marie ought to be out telling people what God had done for her. It was obvious from our previous discussion (although I didn't say it) that he was protecting her, perhaps too much, because of her speech difficulties. He thanked me for the advice and we went on to other subjects.

I next saw them at the LEFE Bible College early in October 1975. Herman, as Dean, had invited me to speak in the chapel with him

The Miracles

and his wife. The change in Marie was profound. She was radiantly beautiful and her speech was faultless. I could hardly believe the difference in the short months since we had last been together.

I asked them about it after the service and they told me that, after what I had said to them at our earlier meeting, they began to realize that Herman was indeed being overprotective of Marie and that she should get out and give her testimony as often as it seemed the Lord wanted. Soon she became quite active as a speaker, and, as she did, her speech cleared up perfectly. Incidentally, in many of the meetings at which she and Herman had spoken, people who asked for prayer were healed.

Before I conclude this chapter I would also like to relate some things Herman said in that chapel service that I hadn't known before. He confessed to the difficult struggle he had had when he realized that the Holy Spirit was asking him to abandon medical treatment for Marie. He was so afraid that he might be making the wrong decision. And he only made that step of faith after real anguish and surrender.

I reflected that, in Herman and Marie's case, her healing depended on his faith and obedience. It is not always so and I'm not sure I know why. It may have something to do with the fact that the Rosenberger's were seriously committed Christians who were not ignorant of God's power and willingness to heal. Whatever the reason, there are times when an answer to prayer is dependent on our trustful obedience, whether it be to remove a brace, to stand in a service, to go to a meeting, or to come home from a hospital.

In any event, the Rosenberger's neurosurgeon later said he thought they had made the right decision. He implied that further surgery or chemotherapy might not have helped and she might have died despite medicine's best efforts. Modern medicine has achieved miracles of its own and the Rosenberger's' experience shouldn't diminish our confidence in its practice. But very few of us - especially those of us who are physicians - would deny that there are cases beyond the scope of our present knowledge or capabilities.

Today Herman is back in the pastorate, serving a large congregation in the San Fernando Valley. In fact, the day I spoke with them to the students of LIFE Bible College was the same day Herman announced his resignation and intent to re-enter the pastoral ministry. I think any church would indeed be fortunate to be served by such a radiant couple whose lives have so evidently been touched by God.

Comment:

Three things make this case an especially excellent example of divine healing:

1. The medical documentation of the case includes biopsy proof of the malignant nature of the brain tumor. The slides were obtained from Hollywood Community Hospital and reviewed the head pathologist at Long Beach Community Hospital who confirmed the diagnosis of malignant astrocytoma or glioma, class II.

2. When the healing occurred, Marie Rosenberg was down to 101 pounds and was expected to die. When Herman Rosenberger called for a night of prayer, his own faith was at an all-time low. He even told his mother-in-law that he felt Marie was going to die. In this state of childlike helplessness, God said she would be healed from the top of her head to the soles of her feet. Her recovery, which started that night and was manifest the following morning, followed in precisely the way it had been prophesied. She received no further drugs or medical therapy from

that time. At the point of desperation, her only treatment was given by the Holy Spirit.

3. The third feature that merits attention in this case is the duration of the healing. Her original craniotomy and diagnosis of malignant brain tumor was May 1970, and she was healed the following year in August. Today, this lady is happy, well and leads an active life. I recently appeared on a telecast with her and her husband at CBS in Hollywood, and she is the picture of health.

Chapter 4

Multiple Sclerosis

Mrs. Marion Burgio

MRS. MARION BURGIO HAD MULTIPLE SCLErosis; and she had seen multiple doctors including more than one neurologist. They all gave their diagnoses on the bases of clinical findings and impressions.

Doctors have been diagnosing this puzzling ailment for almost 150 years. It is a condition of the nervous system. The word, sclerosis, means "hardening." Neurologists have investigated it intensely but there is little agreement concerning the exact diagnosis and specific treatment. In spite of the immense volume of literature reporting about and trying to evaluate multiple sclerosis, many of its mysteries remain unsolved. Its

The Miracles

cause remains unknown, and few can agree about what we should do to treat it properly.

Mrs. Burgio's story is typical of many who have suffered the ravages of this disease. On Tuesday, April 8, 1975, during the annual meeting of the American College of Physicians in San Francisco, I took an afternoon off to visit Mrs. Burgio and her lovely family in the Walnut Creek area. Present for the interview with Mrs. Burgio were her husband, Angelo, and her fourteen-year-old son, Eugene.

When was your first attack?

When I was pregnant with my first child about twenty-nine years ago.

How old are you now?

Fifty-eight.

Was it diagnosed as MS in those early days?

No, they didn't know what it was. I kept falling all the time and I used to pass out when I was pregnant. It all started in 1958. I had numbness in my hands. I'd pick things up and drop them. We were living in Oakland and were both working. The girls noticed a change in my walk and my feet. I went to different doctors and they told me it was poor circulation. But I continued dropping things. And I couldn't control my bladder.

I couldn't keep from bumping into doors and hurting myself. I used to go upstairs and thought I was picking up my feet, but I wasn't, and down I'd go. The car kept stalling when I drove, and Angelo would take it out and say that there was nothing wrong with it. We finally discovered I was not giving it the gas when I thought I was. I took things out of the oven without a pad, and my bath water was so hot it would burn my feet.

Then, in 1962, I began having trouble with my vision. Angelo took me to a doctor in San Francisco and he finally said he didn't know what it was.

Who made the diagnosis?

I entered Memorial Hospital after that and they called in a neurologist who told me I had multiple sclerosis. He was always looking in on me to ask how I was doing. I was deteriorating steadily.

When was the last time that a neurologist was called in to see you?

At John Muir Hospital in 1971.

Did he confirm the diagnosis?

Yes.

Was a spinal tap done at this time?

I think so. I used to have terrible headaches, especially when I had those spinal things.

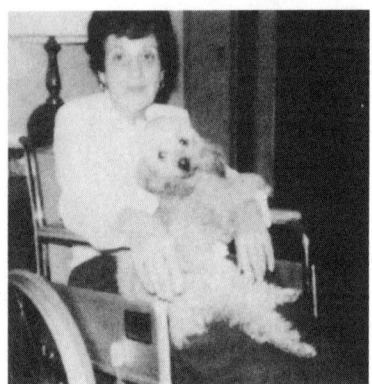

Figure 10: Mrs. Burgio during her illness, confined to a wheelchair, obviously in poor condition.

Figure 11: Mrs. Burgio at her home on April 8, 1975. To her left is her son, Eugene, and husband, Angelo. Her daughter and son-in-law are on her right.

You said that you had a deformity of your left forearm.

When did that flare up?

In 1973.

Was it constant?

At first it came and went, but later it was constant.

Did you ever want to die during your illness?

Yes, I did. Especially the last time.

Did you ever pray to be taken?

At first I wanted to live to raise Eugene and I used to say, Lord, if you just spare me 'til I raise Eugene. But my last time in the hospital, when I knew I couldn't eat or keep my head up, I said, "Lord, take me."

Had you ever considered doing something yourself to end it all?

No. But I used to say, "I'm a nobody here, I feel so useless just plunked on the couch or in the chair. What am I doing around here?"

What happened in the last years when you suffered so?

I wasn't doing too well. Ang kept taking me for injections. In July 1974, I was in Doctors' Hospital in San Leandro for the last time. My stomach was bad, I had a nasty ulcer. I couldn't take aspirin or ACTH shots because it further irri-

The Miracles

tated my stomach. A friend, Helen, came to visit and said, "Marion, I'm gonna pray for you." When she did, I felt my big toe on the right foot move and I heard a beautiful choir in my right ear. Helen told me I was going to be healed. Two days later the doctor came in and said that they had discovered lumps in my throat and started putting tubes down my throat. Twelve days later I went to the healing service.

I don't remember much about the trip. I was too weak even to sit in a wheelchair. My vision and hearing were bad. And that choir was singing in my head all the time! For twelve days it drove me mad! People would ask me what the choir was singing. It was beautiful but I didn't know the name, I had never heard it before.

Tell me about Helen Smith. Is she a mystical individual?

We were neighbors about twenty-five years ago and then we moved and lost contact with each other. I don't remember seeing her for eleven years until their fiftieth anniversary in June 1974. She's in her seventies. We all went. Rosemary came with Dad and me, and the boys went on their own. While Angelo and the boys helped me out of the car,

Rosemary went to the door and Helen said, "Oh, honey, your mother is gonna be healed." She said the same thing to us but we thought maybe she had too much champagne.

She mentioned a prayer meeting and I said, "I don't want to hear about prayer meetings."

Was it after this she came to the hospital to visit you?

Yes. Four or five weeks later she came and prayed, and I told her I heard the choir.

I came home the twenty-second of July and I received a card from Helen telling me she'd take me to the Kathryn Kuhlman service and for me to accept my healing when it came. I didn't know what she was talking about. On the twenty-ninth we got a phone call and a card telling Ang to get me there early, which way to go, and that wheelchairs go in first.

The next morning was the worst of my life. I could barely see, my whole body was shaking, and my hand was twisted terribly. I told Ang, "I'm not going."

"Maybe you'll feel better later."

Both of our TVs went out, my only entertainment. The repairman said he

The Miracles

would have to take both sets out. I was lying there and Ang said, "Get dressed."

"I don't want to go."

Helen told us to be at the coliseum by 3:30 that afternoon. Somehow Angelo finally got me there. We were seated in the wheelchair section and the service began. I don't remember much about it, but, all of a sudden, I found myself on my feet! My hands went out straight, the shakes stopped, I could see, I could hear, my body wasn't crooked, I was straight. I looked down at my feet and they were straight. I started moving and discovered I could walk. I was suddenly in a completely different state of life. I don't remember hearing or saying anything.

Don't you remember anything before that?

I remember complaining to Angelo that I was hot. He took my sweater off, but after a while I got a chill and he put it back on me. Then I was hot again and he said, "You just keep your sweater on."

How long did that go on?

Maybe an hour or so. I thought I had a fever.

What medication had you taken before going?

Darvon compound, Valium, something for the stomach, something for the gas, and thyroid. We had all the pills lined up every morning.

You don't take any of these now?

I had to go back on the thyroid. My eyes got puffy when my doctor took me off them for about six weeks. He took another test. He told me that it showed I still had a thyroid deficiency. I haven't taken one pill otherwise. I'm never tired, I'm going all the time and I do everything. The family can't keep up with me.

Let's go back to the healing service.

I don't know how I got there, but I was on the platform and Miss Kuhlman said, "You're heated honey, you're healed! Walk! " I told her I felt very weird, and she laughed. Then she talked to my husband and he fell to the floor under the power of the Spirit. I didn't know what had happened to him.

What did it feel like, Angelo?

Something like a free-fall. Very pleasant. And I was healed of my bursitis. I had it in my shoulder. A doctor had given me cortisone shots, but I was never able to lift my arm up. My wife used to try to help me put my jacket on. But the next morning, as I was leaving, my wife saw me put my jacket on and said, "You must have had a healing too!"

The Miracles

I moved my arm and said, "By golly, I'm healed!"

But we got more than healing for our bodies that day. I learned that our Lord Jesus Christ is my Savior. I didn't know He was so real. He showed Himself to me.

What do you mean, Marion?

It was something I had never experienced. I felt like I was on a cloud. I knew a power that I had never before experienced touched me. I wasn't dreaming anymore. I started to thank Miss Kuhlman, but she said to thank Jesus.

I confessed to her that I had thought she was a farce and that I had only come to please my friends, Helen and Fred Smith. Miss Kuhlman hollered, "Fred and Helen, where are you, stand up!" They were in the choir and Helen said, "Here I am," and I said, "Hi! " I knew then that I had my voice.

Miss Kuhlman told us to go to the mike and tell everybody whom we were. I said I was Marion Burgio of Walnut Creek, and I went to St. John Vianney Church.

From that night I haven't shut my mouth or sat down. The Lord took away all my shyness and made me bold. For example, a lady called and wanted to know how much I was getting paid to say I was healed. She thought I had been hypnotized. Ang said to hang up. But I talked to her for about an hour and a half. When she said good night she said she had gotten her faith back. I can talk and talk about our Lord Jesus Christ and why we have to adore and praise Him all the time.

That night when we started home we walked all around the parking lot. Ang was pushing Eugene in the wheelchair and people were just hugging me and praising the Lord. They were white, black, hippies, all just sharing God's love with me. When we got home I dialed Helen and Fred to thank them. Helen was in bed already but was still praising the Lord. I called my daughter and told her I was healed. She thought I had gone crazy and told me to go to bed and not talk about it until the next day.

"But honey, I am healed! I can talk. Listen, don't I sound good? I walked all around the coliseum."

"Mother, please."

Then my son-in-law said, "Your mother what?"

"Put daddy on."

"Well, first I have to tell you that

The Miracles

daddy went down gripped in the power of the Spirit."

"He what?!! Who was there?"

"Oh, about 15,000 people."

"Oh, my God, anybody I know?"

"Rosemary, this is daddy, your mother is healed!"

"All right dad, I'll see you tomorrow." The next morning my daughter came, but not alone. She thought, "My mother's gonna be hanging onto things and trying to look healed." She couldn't take it alone, so she asked a neighbor to come with her. When I opened the door her friend looked at me and started crying. My daughter said, "Look at your legs, they're straight!"

"Yes, I told you I was healed of everything." Rosemary sat there for a couple of hours and couldn't open her mouth.

A neighbor called and asked for me. I said, "This is Marion."

"Come on, get off it, I want to talk to Marion."

"El, this is me."

"Marion? What happened to you?"

"I was healed!"

"You were what? I'll be right over." This went on with all my neighbors.

A week later I went to the doctor. I had to see if I was due to go back to the hospital. The appointment was at Doctors' Hospital. Rosemary and I went together.

The girl who had been doing my x-rays for the last two years, Betty, has an aunt who has M.S. Every time we were together she would tell me about her aunt, and how she was doing. Just before I came home from the hospital I went in for x-rays and Betty had given me that little milkshake you take before the x-rays. This was the first we had been together since then and when she saw me she said, "So you have a twin sister."

"Betty, get off it...it's me, Marion."

"What happened? Come in here." She grabbed me, brought me into the x-ray room and shut the door. I told her what happened and she said, "Well, I believe. You know, I wish the doctor who has been taking all your x-rays was here, but unfortunately he's not coming in today." Just as she said that, the door opened and in he walked. He looked at me but didn't say anything. Every few minutes he would look at me while he started taking the x-rays. Betty busied herself around the room and tried not to show her amusement at the doctor's consternation.

Finally he spoke up, "Do you have

The Miracles

pain in your stomach?"

"I don't anymore, but I used to."

"You used to? Did you have an ulcer?"

"Yes, remember, about twelve days ago, I had an ulcer.

"You don't have any pains?"

"No, I'm healed."

"You're healed?"

"Yes, I don't have any more ulcer."

Betty said, "Remember, doctor, a few days ago we had to hold the glass for her to drink the barium?"

He didn't say anything after that, and shortly he gave up, took off his apron and walked out. I said, "Goodbye doc!" We laughed and I told Betty I was sure he wouldn't find anything.

Betty wasn't so sure. "You'd better sit down in the waiting room anyway." I sat there happy as could be and all at once I could see from where I was sitting that they were all pretty busy getting records out of the files. A couple of the girls in the office kept looking at me strangely. I said to Rosemary, "They must think I'm a freak."

Pretty soon the word came, "Mrs. Burgio, get dressed and go home." Next I went to my doctor's office in the front building of the hospital. My doctor said,

"Where's your chair?"

"I don't need it."

"Where's your cane?"

"I don't need it, I'm healed."

Just then he was distracted by a call from the doctor who had just finished taking x-rays of me. I heard him say to his nurse, "Get me all of Mrs. Burgio's records." He was gone for an hour going over all my records. Finally he came back and said, "You don't have any more ulcer, I guess you're healed."

"I know it, I told you."

"I suppose you're going to tell me that your MS is healed too. "

"Right!

Comment

Mrs. Burgio's case presents an example of what I call the full-healing syndrome. There are typically five features of hearings of this sort:

There is usually, but not always, a friend or relative of the patient who feels a burden for their healing. In this story we have Helen, who was involved in the Charismatic Movement in the Catholic Church. She sensed that Marion would be healed and urged her to attend the healing service at the Oakland Coliseum. Helen visited Marion in the hospital to pray for her. Much to Marion's

The Miracles

surprise, a tingling sensation developed in the big toe of her right foot and she began to hear a hymn in her deaf ear. The hymn persisted in this right ear until the day of her healing. At the Oakland Coliseum that afternoon the choir started to sing the hymn, "How Great Thou Art." Marion was startled and said, "That's it, that's the song that has been going through my head."

The second common characteristic is the correction of the physical deformity caused by the illness. In this case there was marked deformity after twelve years of recurrent and persistent multiple sclerosis. At the time of her healing Marion was too weak to stand, she had deformity of two of her extremities, including marked deformity and twisting of the left upper extremity. She had lost control of her bowel and bladder and wore diapers, a humiliating experience for any cognoscent adult. She had extremely poor vision plus double vision, and marked hearing loss in the right ear. When Marion was literally raised from her chair, during the meeting at the Oakland Coliseum, all of these abnormalities instantly disappeared. The severely deformed left upper extremity sprung around into place like a rubber band.

The next common feature of miraculous hearings is spiritual healing. I refer to a change in the personality and the spirit of the individual. Marion's personality changed completely. She had been shy and now she had a new boldness to go forward and preach the Gospel of the Lord Jesus Christ. Marion felt a new closeness with God, and Christ became a reality, not a theological concept.

Typically, those who have been miraculously healed start teaching and talking about Jesus. Marion quickly began giving her testimony to various church groups. She has a prayer meeting in her house once a week and counsels inquirers over the telephone almost every night of the week. She had a third telephone installed in her home because of her expanding ministry to others.

When I visited her home she showed me letters from professional men in various parts of the country asking for her help and counsel because of their own physical and spiritual needs. Marion had not gone beyond the eighth grade and she gave the glory to God that He was using her to help educated, professional people

5. The fifth feature is that when miraculously healed people give their testimonies before groups, there are spontaneous healings in the audience and souls are saved for the Lord Jesus Christ.

Marion once spoke in a church where the minister told her that he would not allow an altar call. Marion decided to abide by this pol-

The Miracles

icy. She gave her testimony from the pulpit and sat down. She closed her eyes in prayer and saw a vision of God. When she opened her eyes, a crowd of people had come forward around the podium for salvation. Thus it is in the lives of those touched by God. Where the Holy Spirit is, there will be His gifts, including faith, hearings and miracles.

Chapter 5

Arteriosclerotic Heart Disease

Mr. Marvin Bird

*A*RTERIOSCLEROTIC HEART DISEASE IS THE most common cause of death in the civilized world. In the United States about one million "coronaries" occur annually. Consequently it has been the subject of intensive medical investigation, and sophisticated diagnostic techniques have been developed for it.

Marvin Bird had his first heart attack in 1956. He was forty-six and a businessman in Lancaster, California. After he suffered two more attacks, his doctor told him either to sell his business or get a new doctor. Mr. Bird sold his business and moved to the Los Angeles area. But his heart disease went with him and he continued to have recurrent chest pains. Mr. Bird was hospitalized for his heart condition seventeen times in sixteen years.

Late in 1970 his cardiologist referred him to the Long Beach VA Hospital for heart catheterization and coronary angiographic study. The following January he entered that institution and, in March, underwent a coronary angiogram. The angiographic study revealed, in the opinion of the doctors who studied it at that time, a complete occlusion of one of his coronary arteries (the left anterior descending) and fifty percent occlusion of the other two. Figure 12 reveals the angiographic appearance upon injection of the left coronary artery. This shows, in all probability, a complete closure of the left anterior descending artery and significant narrowing of the circumflex artery (branch of the left coronary artery). Figure 13 shows the right coronary artery that has some narrowing but significantly less than the left coronary artery branches.

Doctors advised Mr. Bird to undergo coronary artery bypass surgery. He refused because he did not think he would live through it. Thereafter, he declined steadily. His chest pain grew worse and his body grew weaker. In 1972 another group of cardiologists in Long Beach advised him to permit them to operate. Mr. Bird again refused for the same reason. They argued that he had nothing to lose, which would imply that they believed if he did not have the surgery he would not live long anyway.

After he left that hospital he was confined to bed most of the time, too weak to even roll over. He had chest pain more or less continuously. Initially, whenever he developed chest pain, he would try a Nitroglycerin and if that did not relieve the pain he would take Darvon. That failing, he would proceed to Percodan and if that didn't bring relief he resorted to some form of a parenteral narcotic. In addition, his doctors also prescribed Lanoxin, Isordil and Internal.

Mr. Bird had two vivid dreams during this critical time. One night he dreamed that he saw his deceased father and brother-in-law coming over a hill toward him, beckoning him to join them. The night before he attended the Shrine Auditorium, he dreamed that he secured an apartment for his cousin in Iowa. The building, number 315, stood out in his memory of it. The next day, November 19, 1972, at 3:15 in the afternoon, he was suddenly healed of all heart problems.

It was his wife, Amy, who insisted he visit the Shrine that Sunday. She took him into the auditorium by wheelchair. He had taken pain

The Miracles

pills to fortify himself. During the service, Amy Bird suddenly felt exquisite heat in her head that filtered down through her body. It felt, in her words, glorious and put her into a near-trance for some time. She awoke from this to see Maggie Harmer (Miss Kuhlman's assistant) standing over them. After a brief discussion, Maggie asked Marvin Bird to stand up. He did immediately, something previously

impossible for him. Without any bodily sensation he was immediately restored to full health and strength. He later strode out of the Shrine while friends chased him with his wheelchair. He took his wife out to dinner that night for the first time in a long time. His appetite was vigorous. He stayed up until past midnight that night watching television. After a sound sleep he awakened feeling healthy and robust. He has had n o chest pain nor has he taken any medication for his heart since that day in November 1972.

Excerpts from an interview with Mr. & Mrs. Marvin Bird, Wednesday April 2, 1975 at their home.

Are these the medications you were on?

Yes, sir. Lanoxin .25mg, Isordil 2.5 mg, Inderal 10 mg.

How often were you on Inderal, do you remember?

It was too long for me to remember.

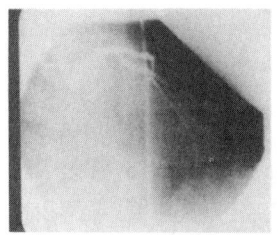
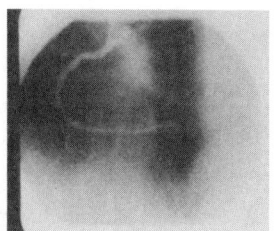

Figure 12: *Injection of Marvin Bird's left coronary artery indicated probable complete occlusion of the left anterior descending artery and significant narrowing of the left circumflex artery.*

Figure 13: *Injection of Mr. Bird's right coronary artery indicated that it was narrowing somewhat. It is, however, significantly less involved with the atheromatous process than the branches of the left coronary artery.*

Figure 14: *This photograph was taken shortly before Mr. Bird attended the Shrine Auditorium on the day of his hearing.*

Figure 15: *This photograph shows Mr. & Mrs. Marvin Bird after his hearing.*

The Miracles

Tell me about your first attack in 1956.

I was doing some work on my lawn, it was heavy work and I passed out. There might have been a lapse of time, but I managed to get up and go in the house. I was not going to tell Amy, but she saw I was very ill and took me to the hospital. It was the first of many trips over the next years. The diagnosis was arteriosclerotic heart disease manifested by angina pectoris and prolonged circulation time.

In 1970 you had a left heart cath and coronary arteriogram. You were hospitalized in Hoague Hospital once and also once in Minneapolis.

I became very ill at my sister's home in Minneapolis and they couldn't reach a doctor. The fire department came and administered oxygen. My sister called the ambulance and I was taken to General Hospital, intensive care. The work-up started in the morning and I was there about ten or twelve weeks. They took the angiogram and decided that I should have open-heart surgery, which I declined.

One of your arteries was completely plugged off.

The doctors gathered around my bed and one of them drew on the back of an envelope to show me that the middle artery was completely blocked and the others were narrowed about fifty percent.

Tell me about your healing.

We went to the Shrine Auditorium. During the service Maggie Harmer realized there was a healing in our area and was trying to find it. Finally she asked me to stand up. When I had been taken in there, two ushers had to help Amy get me out of my wheelchair. But now I stood up. There was no problem, no pain. I felt wonderful, but I did not go up on the platform with Miss Kuhlman because I could not believe. I knew miracles could happen, but not to me, so I sat down. And as I sat down I brushed my sleeve across my watch and the time was 3:15. Only later did I associate that with my dream about the apartment for my cousin in Iowa.

Let's go back to the time leading up to your healing.

My condition was getting worse all the time.

And the doctors said you might as well have the surgery, that you might die if you didn't?

I had nothing to lose. The last attack was on a Friday, the thirteenth of

The Miracles

October. I was driving home along Beach Boulevard and had to pull over and take a Nitroglycerin. The pains were terrific. A police officer came along and asked me what was the matter. I told him I just had a little dizzy spell. However, I knew I had a bad attack and, when I got home, I took all my medication. I took Darvon, I took Percodan, I took everything I had and couldn't suppress the pain.

Amy called the fire department rescue squad. They definitely wanted to get me into the hospital and called the ambulance. I was taken to the VA that night and they sent me up to the eleventh floor to intensive care again. They did a lot of work that night, taking a gas test. They were going to my wrists. I was in intensive care for a while. I don't know how many days later I was released down to the tenth floor.

One of the doctors who attended me had examined the astronauts before they went into space. He was in charge of that cardiac ward. They tried to convince me I had nothing to lose, that I might make it. But they would not talk percentages.

When did you come home?

My family brought me home a few

days after that. That's the last time I was in a hospital. I came home to die. I quit eating. My medication didn't really help. I couldn't turn over in bed. Friends started coming just to stay a little while and go. Many of them never expected to see me alive again.

Tell me more about what happened to you at the Shrine Auditorium.

Maggie Harmer was looking for a healing. She asked Amy who among us needed a healing, and Amy pointed to me. Maggie asked me what my problem was. I told her my heart.

"Don't you feel stronger?"

"What?"

"Stand up." If you'd held a thousand dollar bill out in front of me, I couldn't have gotten it. But I stood up!

This was at 3:15, and then what? Did you sit out the rest of the service?

Yes, we witnessed the other miracles. We'd never been to one before; we didn't know what this was all about.

Then you came home?

Oh, I was hungry! I hadn't eaten for quite some time. So we went to Villa Sweden. It is owned by a Christian family and they are very close to us. I ate Swedish meatballs with all the trimmings. When we came home, Amy

The Miracles

couldn't get me to bed. I was too excited. I hadn't been able to get out of my bed to watch TV before, so I sat there enjoying the programs till 12:30 that night. The next morning I thought it would be all over, but I got out of bed with no problem, had breakfast, walked around, looked at my car. The next day I got in my car, and Amy and I both went down to the supermarket and bought groceries, bags of groceries!

The third day I was still going strong, so I called my doctor. Now you just can't drop in and see him, you have to make an appointment weeks before. But he told me to come right in. In the examining room I stripped to the waist as usual. The doctor came in. He looked at me and backed up,

"Why, Marv, what's happened? You look wonderful!"

I wasn't gonna tell him anything. He went all over my chest with that stethoscope and then checked back in my records. He looked at the records and me. A week before my pulse was forty-eight which I understand is pretty slow. Now it was seventy-two. Finally he just shook my hand and wished me a Merry Christmas. Later, when I was on the stage to tell my story to Kathryn

Kuhlman, I said I must have left him in a state of shock because he didn't charge me for the office call. Kathryn said, "There's a miracle!"

What else happened after your healing?

When the medical profession confirmed that I was healed, really accepted the fact that a miracle happened to me. It was so wonderful that I just had to believe in God. And that's when we went to church. After the service I was up in front with the pastor and said I would like to give my life to Christ. I felt good. People came up to the altar to kiss and hug me.

How have you been changed since that?

There is never a day that I do not thank God for what happened. We go to church and listen to Christian programs on TV. Amy and I enjoy taking people to a miracle service. The time we counted, there must have been twenty-seven people we had taken to Kathryn Kuhlman services, several of whom were healed. We took another couple we'd known for ten years, but we did not know they were on the verge of a divorce. She confided in Amy later that they became reconciled and are living a normal life. There's an example of an emotional healing; all hearings are not physical.

The Miracles

One man testified at the Shrine Auditorium that he had had open-heart surgery and was at home recuperating in bed. He had given up, and did not expect to live. Then he saw a man on Miss Kuhlman's telecast that also had a serious problem with his heart. He called his wife into the bedroom and they watched the telecast together. It gave him so much faith that he was healed in his home. It made me especially happy because I was the one on that telecast. Another time I gave my testimony at a Catholic prayer meeting and while sharing my experience, a lady, who had had brain damage at birth and suffered with seizures ever since, was healed. She was on heavy medication and from that night she never took her medication and never had a seizure.

Have you seen her since then?

Yes, many times. She has been back to her doctor, but used no medication for nine months. Her husband had to give up his work six months before that meeting because of a heart condition. He did not receive an instant healing but, a few days after that, he was out changing the tires on his car and doing all the things he never dreamed he would be able to do. People don't have to go to a Kathryn Kuhlman service to be cured, it can happen any time.

Amy Bird's story is an interesting sidelight that further illuminates this chronicle of her husband's healing. She had attended Marvin during his illness and, during the week preceding their visit to the Shrine Auditorium when Marvin was so ill, Mrs. Bird was becoming quite exhausted. She had often been up at night with Marvin because he was too weak to get water to take oral medications.

On Thursday night of that week, Amy was awakened by a painful ailment of her own. Forgetting about her own problems, she slipped out of bed and went to an adjacent room where she could pray quietly. She got on her knees and prayed as she had never prayed before. A peace came over her that she had not previously known and she felt the presence of the Lord Jesus. He spoke to her and said that Marvin would be all right.

In the morning Marvin seemed slightly improved with less chest pain. He changed his mind and agreed to go to the Shrine Auditorium service. Before they entered the auditorium a feeling of power came over Amy. It was difficult for her to describe, but it was accompanied by tranquility and a reassurance that all would be well.

The Miracles

During the service, when she felt heat go over her, her painful ailment was relieved and has not recurred. In addition, two days after the Shrine service her sinuses suddenly started clearing and she has had no recurrence of this difficulty since then.

Since the service she has felt a deep peace and, although she was a religious person, she found a new desire to read the Bible and a heightened interest in things of the Spirit. She also has a strong desire to witness to others.

Comment

Mr. Bird's healing clearly illustrates all the features of a complete healing syndrome.

Mr. Bird's wife encouraged him to attend a healing service. Of interest is the fact that Mr. Bird had no sensation when he was healed although his wife did. Mr. Bird had taken pain medication just before the service and I wonder if this might have been the reason. One of the other patients in this series, Mrs. Elfrieda Stauffer, took pain medication prior to the service in which she was healed, and also experienced no sensation at the time of her healing.

Mr. Bird was instantaneously restored to vigorous health from nearly total invalidism.

The full impact of the spiritual healing was not felt in Marvin Bird's life until a week after the Shrine service when he went forward to receive Christ following a service at a nearby church.

During the three years since his healing, Mr. Bird has been speaking, teaching, and giving his testimony before various groups. During several of these occasions, healings have been reported to occur in the audience.

Many of the cases described in this book have included prophetic visions or dreams. The night before he was healed Mr. Bird had a dream in which he lost the key to his cousin's apartment. While they searched for the key, they had to put the pieces of a puzzle back together at an address numbered 315. At 3:15, God put the pieces of Marvin Bird's health puzzle back together.

Figure 16: *Mr. B. Ray Jackson*

Chapter 6

Carcinoma of the Kidney (Hypernephroma) With Diffuse Bony Metastases

Mr. B. Ray Jackson

RAY JACKSON ENTERED THE DUKE UNIVERSITY Medical Center on Monday, December 19, 1972. The physician who worked him up on the urologic service noted the following: This was the first DUMC admission for this forty-three year old bank executive who on December 16, 1972 had had painless gross hematuria (blood in the urine). He had first gone to the emergency room of a local hospital in Jacksonville, North Carolina, near his home, and was treated with antibiotics. The next day he had more hematuria and colicky pain. On the 18th of December

The Miracles

1972, his personal physician performed an intravenous pyelogram (kidney x-ray). This study revealed a left renal mass. The doctor quickly referred him to the urologic department at Duke for evaluation and treatment.

At the time of admission he was taking Percodan for pain. He had no drug sensitivities and no history of blood transfusions. As a child, he had had his tonsils and adenoids removed. Nothing in his personal or family medical history would have led one to suspect he might have cancer of the kidney (renal carcinoma) or kidney stones. Physical examination revealed that his blood pressure was a little above normal, but he was well developed and nourished, and in no acute distress.

In the hospital he underwent an abdominal aortogram and selective left renal, right renal and celiac arteriograms which revealed a hypernephroma (cancer) of the left kidney with no evidence of extra-renal involvement. On Thursday, December 22nd, surgeons performed a left radical nephrectomy (removed his left kidney). Postoperatively the patient did well. By the seventh postoperative day his drains and sutures were removed and he was discharged from the hospital. As an outpatient, the doctors prescribed iron sulfate and antibiotic for a urinary tract infection from which Mr. Jackson promptly recovered.

Pathologists examined the kidney after it was removed and confirmed that its tumor was indeed malignant, an adenocarcinoma.

The patient returned home, carried on his normal activities, and did well until February 1974, when he noted soreness in his left ring finger. X-rays showed a destructive lesion of the proximal phalanx (bone), which was thought (and subsequently proved) to be metastatic carcinoma. That meant that cancer cells from that tumor in his left kidney had probably escaped into his bloodstream before the operation and taken up residence in his finger. This is the thing every surgeon dreads in trying to eradicate cancer from a patient. There is a critical time period with malignant tumors after which they begin to emit cells into the rest of the body. These cells travel through the bloodstream, the lymphatic vessels, or along membranous surfaces, find resting places, as in Mr. Jackson's finger, and begin producing new carcinomas.

Surgeons removed his finger on March 4th and doubtless kept their own fingers crossed that this was the only metastatic lesion he would suffer. Lab reports confirmed that the finger did contain metastatic clear cell carcinoma. It was unlikely that only one cell had escaped from that kidney before they removed it, but they could hope so until the evidence went against them, which it did.

The Miracles

In less than two months Mr. Jackson came back to the hospital complaining of soreness in the right anterior chest and left inguinal area (groin). Plane x-ray showed a destructive lesion in the inferior ischial ramus on the left (pelvic bone). A bone scan revealed multiple hot spots, including the sternum (breastbone), the spine (T-12-L-1), the right sacroiliac joint, the right fibula (lower leg bone), and, as in the x-ray, the left ischial ramus (see figures 17 and 18). The worst had happened. Surgery was out of the question. The only hope might be in hormone and radiation therapy.

The doctors prescribed Provera, a hormone, and recommended radiation therapy to the left ischium (pelvic bone) for relief of pain. The radiologists discussed the other areas in his skeleton to which metastatic cancer had spread and told him there was little hope that he would live another year. They released him on April 26, 1974, to spend a weekend at home with his family and scheduled him to return to the medical center the following Monday to begin radiation therapy. When he did return, however, they decided against it.

Ray Jackson reported that his pain had disappeared. He was evidently healed. He was sent home and resumed his normal activities. He returned to Duke University Medical

Center in October for a checkup. The physician made the following note in the medical records:

> This 45-year-old bank executive had a left nephrectomy in December 1972 following hematuria and histologic diagnosis was adenocarcinoma. Following painful swelling of the left fourth finger, x-rays in March 1974 demonstrated metastatic disease and on March 4th the digit was amputated confirming the radiologic impression. By late April he had severe pains in the right anterior rib cage and in the left ischium. A bone scan showed abnormalities in the sternum at T-12-L-1, in the left pelvis, in the right S-1 joint and in the fibula. Provera therapy was initiated 30 mg a day.
>
> Within one week on initiating Provera therapy and following a religious experience in Florida when he went to see Kathryn Kuhlman, all pain subsided and irradiation therapy which had been planned for the left ischium was not given. Since then he has felt quite well without pain, cough, shortness of breath, weight loss, or intercurrent illness.
>
> Skeletal survey showed remarkable "healing" of the lesion in the left

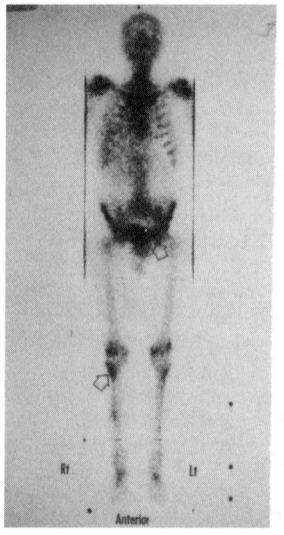
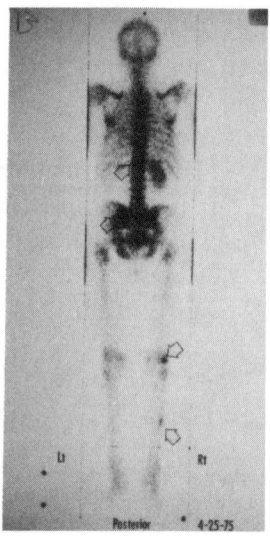

Figure 17: *This is a total body bone scan from the front of Mr. Jackson, made in April 1974. The arrows point to apparent tumors in the skeleton, which clinicians observe as "hot spots" in this procedure.*

Figure 18: *This is a total body bone scan taken from the back of Mr. Jackson in April 1974. The arrows indicate more hot spots.*

ischium and similar increase in density in a former lytic site in the medial portion of the left ileum.

During that same October visit, Ray Jackson was subjected to a metastatic survey, x-rays of the bones including all long bones. The x-ray department reported the following:

> The current examination including a lateral view of the skull, AP and lateral views of the spine, AP view of the pelvis and views of the proximal humeri and femora were compared with representative prior radiographs. *Healing* is noted of the previously described metastatic focus in the left ischium. No other metastatic foci can be identified. Despite the history afforded of a positive bone scan in the T-12-L-1 area in the left pelvis and right sacroiliac joints, no definite metastatic foci can be seen in these regions.

The diagnosis on this lab report was as follows:

1. Healing of the previously described metastatic focus of the left ischium.
2. No other metastatic foci are identified.

The Miracles

A return note by a member of the urologic department dated 10/17/74 stated the following:

> The patient states after I last saw him he apparently had bone scans that showed five different lesions involving the ribs and part of the pelvis. They were apparently metastatic. He was initially going to receive cobalt therapy but over a weekend he went to some religious revival and his pain disappeared. He came back on the following day and on May 1 St, he was put on Provera 10 mg t.i.d. and he has been fine since. He had lost over 20 pounds prior to starting the Provera but he has gained all that back and a little more. He is now playing golf, exercises well, feels perfect in general. On examination he looks to be in excellent health.

On May 22, 1975, Mr. Jackson returned to DUMC for another routine check. The physician in the urologic department noted the following:

> The patient is feeling fine. He states he gained so much weight that he discontinued his Provera two months ago. He states he is feeling better than he

ever has in his life. Examination reveals him to look very well. There is no abdominal mass, or tenderness present. Urine is chemically and microscopically negative. Chest x-ray requested. Patient is strongly advised to go back on the Provera... .

On November 17, 1975, a physician in the hematology division of the department of medicine at Duke University Medical Center wrote:

Dear Mr. Jackson:

Dr. - didn't realize that I was to return to clinic shortly when he let you go after your visit on November 13th. I am sorry that time did not permit my reinforcing the encouraging results we found on physical examination.

Careful review of the chest x-ray showed no abnormalities and the chemistry survey was quite healthy as well. There was no abnormality of liver function, renal function, or of the blood calcium.

We can only assume that the neoplasm is in remission, *whatever the reason*. Dr. - told me that he suggested resumption of the Provera compound. It certainly isn't mandatory although its

The Miracles

administration coincided with a remarkable resolution in bone pain and stabilization of the bone scan.

If there are any other ways we can be of assistance, please let us know.

Sincerely, (name withheld)

I would like to permit Mr. Jackson to tell what happened to him over that weekend during which he attended, in the words of one of the doctors, some religious revival:

My wife and I returned home that weekend praying for a miracle. All my Christian friends were fasting and praying with us for the same thing.

I had just completed a book my wife gave me called *I Believe in Miracles* by Kathryn Kuhlman. Jesus had become my Lord and Savior several years before. I knew it would take a miracle from Him to get well and decided to fly my family to Jacksonville, Florida, on Saturday, April 27, 1974, to attend Miss Kuhlman's miracle service on Sunday, the 28th, at 1:00 P. M.

At 4:30 on Sunday morning, I woke up in my motel room, got on my knees, thanked and praised the Lord for where I was, and cried out for a miracle of healing. Suddenly I had a vision of a face. I knew it was Jesus Christ through His Holy Spirit. He told me, in an audible voice, I was going to be healed. I thanked Him again and, at ten minutes to five o'clock, I got back in bed and went to sleep in complete peace.

We arose at 7:30, got dressed, and went to the Gator Bowl Coliseum to attend Miss Kuhlman's miracle service. Over 15,000 people were there praying for everyone's needs to be met, whether they were physical or spiritual. I was the fourth person of hundreds to go up to the altar and Jesus Christ took away the cancer pains instantly. Praise His Holy Name!

I returned to Duke on Monday morning to begin treatments. I told the radiation therapy doctors about my miracle in Florida and of the release of pain from my body. They did not begin therapy, but advised me to return the next morning for another bone scan. That scan showed that the tumors were still there just as in the previous Thursday's scan. I was told to immediately report to radiation therapy and begin treatment. I did, still praising God for the absence of pain, even though I knew, at this point, that radiation and chemotherapy treatments were apparently still necessary. But the doctors called me, and after further consultation and examination, they were convinced I was not experiencing any pain. They released me and told me to return June 13th for examination, and to call them immediately should I start having pain.

By June 13th I had regained my normal weight of 180 pounds and had not missed a day's work. The doctors gave me all the usual tests, x-rays, examinations, etc., and told me the results were very good. They scheduled an appointment for me to return October 17, 1974. At that time all tests, including a complete bone survey, showed that new bone had filled in and all my bones were perfectly smooth in all tumor areas. My wife and doctor joined me in prayer, thanking Jesus for His blessing of healing.

Periodic checks since then have continued to confirm that I am fully healed.

Comment

Ray Jackson's story is notable for the wealth of medical documentation available from the Duke University Medical Center, a prestigious institution by any standards. Dr. Richard Steiner has, as with earlier appropriate cases in this book, reviewed the slides provided by the Duke physicians and confirmed their diagnosis of metastatic cancer to bone.

In a portion of his testimony, which I have not included above, Ray Jackson reports that he began to seek divine healing immediately after he first passed the blood on December 16, 1972. While he waited for his doctor to return his call, he summoned two friends, members of a prayer group he attended, to his home. In Biblical fashion they anointed him with oil, and prayed for healing. Soon many friends and family members were praying.

An elderly uncle called late Saturday evening and urged them to believe God was speaking to them through a Bible passage, Ezekiel 16:6, and to pray that the bleeding would stop. The passage read in part, "I ... saw you weltering in your blood, [and] ... said to you in your blood, 'Live...........' " Bolstered by this they prayed anew and, within an hour, the bleeding stopped. Sunday morning, however, he had severe pain and went to the local hospital emergency ward. The next day he entered DUMC and a few days later his left kidney was removed.

The point of this is that here again we see members of the Christian community encouraging one who is sick to seek healing. This encouragement was culminated a little over a year later when his wife gave him a copy of *I Believe in Miracles* to read in the hospital. Significantly, with the metastatic spread of cancer over various parts of his skeleton, he was then, in effect, beyond the help of medical science. Even with the hormone and radiation therapy, his physicians advised him not to expect to live more than a year, perhaps much less.

In this state of hopelessness he had a vision and soon thereafter, at the Kathryn Kuhlman meeting, felt that he was thoroughly healed because all his pain disappeared. He did, by the way, experience a sensation like electricity running throughout his body during the service. It is especially interesting to have clinical tests on the day following that show that the lesions had not yet disappeared.

This, at first, indicated that radiation therapy was in order, and why the doctors changed their minds and decided to forego it is not altogether clear. They, after all, had, as contrary evidence, only Jackson's word that the pain had disappeared. Ray reports that one of his physicians was a man of some faith, and this may account for it. They could not have attributed any miraculous response to Provera, since he did not fill the prescription nor begin taking it until May 5th, one week after he attended the healing service in

Florida. He kept taking it, incidentally, until December 31st and then quit altogether. Finally, the bone marrow tests, taken April 26th, turned up nothing.

True to form, Mr. Jackson has been telling everyone about his healing since the day it happened. As of July 28, 1975, he had spoken to fifty-five churches, civic clubs, and businessmen's groups, testifying to the power of Jesus Christ, using his own experience to illustrate.

Chapter 7

Mixed Rheumatoid and Osteoarthritis

Pearl Bryant Ph.D.

PEARL BRYANT, AT THE AGE OF SEVENTY-eight, is the oldest person and the only Ph.D. (doctor of speech therapy) in our series. Good medical records document her claims. In 1968 she underwent an extensive examination by several specialists at St. Joseph's Hospital, Kansas City, Missouri. She had a long history of arthritis (first diagnosed at the Mayo Clinic in 1939), particularly in her back and lower extremities, neck and shoulders. And, the records show, she complained of increasing mental slowness during the preceding five or six months.

She also had a long history of kidney

stones and genitourinary problems. She had had a tonsillectomy in 1915, an appendectomy in 1923, retrograde treatment for kidney stones in 1942, with exploration of the kidneys in 1943, and plastic surgery of the left kidney in 1945. This was done in Barnes Hospital, St. Louis, and she was still under the care of her urologist in Kansas City. Doctors removed her gall bladder as well as abscesses on her liver in 1961 at Research Hospital, Kansas City.

In 1961 she also saw an orthopedist who paid particular attention to her knees because of her history of falling on several occasions. His examination revealed "a good deal of arthritis, and partial subluxation of the joint. The patient has fallen a great many times on this left knee." The orthopedist suggested a long-leg brace.

X-ray studies of the left knee and hip were consistent with osteoarthritis with mild decalcification of the skeletal structures. X-ray of the spine showed some inter-body bridging of the lower thoracic spine. Laboratory studies revealed a markedly elevated sedimentation rate of sixty-three, no LE cells were seen, latex agglutination test was non-reactive.

Long-leg braces were applied and for ten years she wore them whenever she was out of bed. During those same years she suffered from a multitude of ailments. She complained, in addition to the usual problems associated with her extensive osteoarthritis and gastrointestinal difficulties, of fainting spells, frequent headaches, swelling of the ankles, nausea, constipation, digestive irregularities, bloating, indigestion, and sore mouth.

Her medical treatment during the time of her illness included injections of ACTH and other steroids including Celestone. On an intermittent basis she took steroids, such as Prednisone, orally. Pain medications included narcotics like Demerol and muscle relaxants like Norflex, which was given by injection. Other medications included Norgesic, Peritrate, antacids, Zentinic, Dorbane or Alophen, Bucladin, Talwin, OsCalmone, Urised, Choloxin, Butibelzyme, Robaxin, Arlidin, Pavabid, injections of vitamins and liver, and flu vaccine.

Pearl Bryant was a devout Methodist who had read the Bible through several times, but she had never thought seriously about asking God to heal her. She was taken to a Kathryn Kuhlman healing service, after reading *God Can Do It Again*. During the service she was healed. After the healing her doctor dictated a note on her medical chart, dated 10/15/74:

> Feels better and is walking without her leg braces since claiming a faith-healing experience; also stopped all her

medications. General condition appears good. Continue no regular medication.

On the next follow-up visit to her physician on December 17th, he dictated another note: *Continues to ambulate without benefit of braces.*

She visited her physician again on May 20, 1975. The doctor noted:

Feels well and has stopped all her medication-Continue no regular medication.

In June 1975, Doctor Bryant came to Los Angeles for a television appearance and to give her testimony at the Shrine Auditorium. A few days later, on June 18th, she came to my office for an interview regarding her illness and healing. I'll let her tell her own story.

I had been retired not quite two years, because the pain had become so severe that I would have muscular spasms and blackouts while I was working with the students.

I couldn't even get into a car without terrific pain in my legs. I'd have to slide back in the seat of the car and then, as I would turn my hips, someone would have to pick up my feet and put them into the car.

H. Richard Casdorph

One day a friend named Ruth brought over some books. Among them was *God Can Do It Again*. As I read it something began to perk. I realized I had never asked God to heal me!

I wore braces. I couldn't bend my knees and, when I fell, I fell full-length because the braces were locked! The licks one gets when one falls forward full-length without anything to cushion it are nasty. My doctors had told me that there was nothing more they could do. Some of my friends had had surgery and new joints put in, but they wouldn't advise it.

My dear doctor said he could only try to keep down the pain. The pain was terrific. So, on September 8, 1974, I asked God to heal me. Then I tried for five consecutive mornings to sit on the side of my bed and stand without putting on my braces. I prayed, tried to walk, and fell. I couldn't take a step without those braces. There was no use trying to overdo it. I decided after the fifth day, that this just wasn't God's plan.

I wasn't bitter about it. Why should He heal me? What is there left for me to do at my age? I gave up and decided to make the best of it. Shortly after that I

The Miracles

began to get the impression that I should go to St. Louis. I couldn't understand it. Why in heaven's name should I go to St. Louis? I would wake up at night and something would be telling me to go to St. Louis. And on the third day, the same friend who had loaned me the book called to invite me to go with her to see Kathryn Kuhlman in St. Louis on September 18th and 19th. I accepted, but I didn't tell her anything about my experience. I don't think she had any idea about me going for the healing. She just wanted us to see Kathryn Kuhlman in the flesh!

We arrived at the auditorium in St. Louis at 4:30 in the afternoon. People were just packed in front of the doors. I hadn't been standing there more than fifteen minutes, when I began to black out. Ruth cried, "Oh, my goodness, what will I do with you?"

"Come on!" I got hold of a rope and we tried to lunge ahead. People stood aside a bit and we came face to face with an usher.

"Lady, lady! You can't come in here. The doors don't open 'til 6:30!"

Ruth said, "What are we gonna do?"

"Lady, lady."

"Let me tell you something, young

man, God told me to come to St. Louis and I've stood here as long as I... . "

I blacked out. The next thing I knew I was inside the building, having muscular spasms. When I began to come back to reality, this dear little usher said, "What am I gonna do with you, lady?"

"I'm going in there."

"I don't think there's a seat on the first floor."

"Then take me up to the balcony."

"Up to the balcony? I don't know how I could ever get you to one of those empty seats."

"Okay, I'll go in that auditorium, I'm going in there if I have to sit on the floor."

I couldn't have sat on that floor with those braces on if I had wanted to, but I was determined to go in.

"Never mind, lady. I'll give you my seat."

His seat was in the middle section next to the last row, on the aisle. I got myself straightened out as much as I could so I wouldn't be as likely to have another attack.

The choir director came out shortly and described the philosophy of Kathryn Kuhlman. He said that there's

The Miracles

one thing many people forget. You must let God do it. It all depends on His mercy alone. You don't need to struggle to help Him. That's why I had to come to St. Louis! I had been trying to take that step, I was trying to help God! I saw how ridiculous I had been. So I relaxed, bowed my head and prayed silently,

"I do have faith in Your mercy. Do with me what You want." Something began to happen over in my left hip. It felt as if a grinder was going around the joint. I thought of the old coffee grinder we used to have when I was a girl. Sometimes it seemed as if it hit something and was having a hard time getting through. It was a sound more than a sensation.

After it had done that for a while, I had the feeling of an electric current going down the outside and the inside of my leg to my knee. When it hit the knee joint, that same grinding that had been at the hip joint started at the knee. I lost all sense of reality. I didn't hear the choir singing. I was virtually in a trance. It was the most peaceful, joyful experience.

That same current-like thing on either side of my leg went to the ankle joint and then passed across my lower back over to the right leg where the same thing happened. It came up my spine and it took the longest time. It was grinding each joint. Then it got up to my shoulders and did the same thing in the left shoulder down to the elbow, wrist, and fingers. Then it went over to my right arm and worked up to my neck. I had been having so much trouble with my neck that the doctor thought it was time for me to put on a permanent brace. I had a holy horror of that. I had been wearing a temporary brace, such as is worn for whiplashes.

Then, according to the man who sat next to me, I exclaimed, "Oh, thank you, God! You're getting my neck!"

And I saw a vision of Jesus in a misty setting, like the garden of Gethsemane. He was smiling at me, He didn't speak but His face assured me that everything was all right. He was wearing a white robe and He touched me on my shoulder and hand. But His face impressed me most. He was smiling. Then I awoke to realize I hadn't heard a song or even the sermon.

The healing service was well underway when I regained consciousness. At first it seemed far away ... someone had his sight restored and someone who had

The Miracles

been deaf in one ear had hearing again. As I really began to become aware of everything, a young fellow ran down the aisle. He had been healed of a very rare disease and he was jubilant.

About that time Kathryn put up her hand, "Someone in the back of this room who's in braces has been healed. Take off those braces and come up and proclaim your Lord!"

I began to look all around. I didn't realize that I had been healed.

There were more healings. Miss Kuhlman put up her hand again, "There is someone way back, if it isn't the back row it's near the back row, who is in braces and has been healed. Take off those braces! Come up and proclaim your Lord!"

I looked all along the back, no response! A third time she said,

"I don't understand, don't you know you can walk? Take off those braces and find out you can walk!"

Finally it dawned on me, and I thought, "I wonder if I can walk? I'm the only one I can see in braces. I can't take the braces off in here because I would have to undress." I motioned for the usher, "Is there a restroom near?"

"Oh, no, lady. I don't see how I could

ever get you to a restroom! Is it an emergency?"

"Forget about it; it's all right."

By that time I had used my head a bit and decided I couldn't get my braces off then and there. I knew I would be back the next night. Meanwhile I did what checking I could to see if I was indeed healed. I had practically no left kneecap from all my trouble, so I felt and it was there! I also had a painful indentation in my left hip. I touched it and didn't feel anything, it wasn't sore!

My excitement grew. I had a pinched nerve in my back, which hurt like the dickens in certain positions so I gave myself a little jerk, a very cautious one, and nothing happened. So I leaned over and I gave a good yank and it didn't hurt and I thought, "I'll bet I am the one who's healed!"

After the dismissal, Ruth found me, "Weren't you healed tonight?"

"Yes, I was healed. I'm sure I could walk if I could get these braces off."

"I can't understand why you didn't go down and proclaim it. What was the matter with you!" She was disgusted.

"How could I get my braces off?"

She leaned against the wall and laughed and laughed, "That didn't even enter my mind. When Miss Kuhlman said that someone with braces in the back had been healed, I knew it was you. I watched and watched for you to go down that aisle and when you didn't, I couldn't understand. It didn't enter my mind that you couldn't take the braces off."

Back at the Holiday Inn everybody was tired. I could hardly wait to walk, but one of the women with us had a heart condition and needed rest, and if I had walked there would not have been any resting that night. So I decided that the next morning I would leave off my braces and walk. And indeed I did! I walked all around my room; I walked down to breakfast and back to the table farthest from the door. I walked!

I planned that morning to look up some of my former students who were working in St. Louis now. We would have to drive across town to a school where they were teaching. The fellow who was our driver said he wouldn't take me unless I put on my braces.

"I'm not going to put on the braces and, if you don't want to take me over, I'll get somebody else."

"Okay. We'll put them in the trunk of the car, but I'm not going without them."

So we went over and I walked from one building to another. I went upstairs and down. I even got into a fire drill by accident and ran along with the rest of them. My friends, however, began to be convinced when we sat down to lunch. The lunchroom tables and the benches were fastened to the floor. I couldn't slide one back and I hadn't raised a foot that high in years. But I had to step over the bench. And I did, and we laughed and visited all during the lunch hour. But my friends were still afraid that I was going to do something that would break a bone.

I was having one problem, though. In those early hours of walking I had no feeling in my legs. I could walk, but I had to look down to see where I was stepping because I didn't have any feeling.

By the way, I had such poor circulation in my legs that for years I had practically no feeling from my waist down. Even when they gave me cortisone with big needles, I couldn't feel it. In order to have enough warmth to sleep at all, I had one electric blanket underneath me, another over me, and an electric pad under my feet. I could stand on the gas heating registers in our home and not feel it. My shoes would burn, but I

The Miracles

couldn't feel the heat.

We went back to the auditorium that afternoon. A large crowd stood out in front as before and Ruth said, "What are you going to do today?"

"I'm waiting my turn with the rest of the people; I'm not special."

"I don't think that's very smart, you have had a hard day. Just about then the same usher spied me, "Yoo-hoo, lady." I ignored him.

"Yoo-hoo, lady! Come on, I have a place for you." People began to step aside to let me through. So I went and, when I got up close, he said, "I saved a seat for you tonight. I didn't want to miss giving it to you... Wait a minute! I thought ... but you are the woman. Weren't you in braces last night?"

"Yes!"

"I don't need to ask, I can tell by looking, you've been healed! We'll have rejoicing tonight!! I'm going right up and tell Miss Kuhlman."

"Oh, no, you're not! You wait till the healing part of the service and then we'll tell Miss Kuhlman." So he took me to the seat he had saved.

When Kathryn came out on the platform, the first thing she said was, "Something has bothered me all day. I don't understand about that person who was here last night in braces, who didn't come up. I hope you're here tonight!"

But I waited until she was ready for the healing part. Then I got up and started down the aisle. The man who was with our group had said he would take the braces and go around to the side door of the auditorium. That way we could show the braces without having to carry them through the crowd. One of the Kuhlman workers stopped me in the aisle to ask what I was doing.

"I've been healed!"

"How do you know?"

"I can walk!"

"Didn't you walk before?"

"Not like this I didn't! I'm the one Miss Kuhlman spoke of who had the braces!"

She couldn't get me up there fast enough after that. On the platform, Kathryn said, "And so you have been healed tonight?"

"No, I was healed last night. I'm the one who was in braces last night and didn't come up."

"Why didn't you?"

"Miss Kuhlman, you're a very great woman and I admire you from the bottom of my heart, but you don't know how people put on and take off full length leg and back braces."

She said, "What? Where are they?" And this fellow held both of the leg braces up.

"You wore those? Can you go get them?" I did and she said, "How did you wear them? Show us."

I showed how they fastened to the bottom of my shoes, how they came up and locked, and so on. And she said, "I don't need to ask you if you've been healed, it shows all over you."

Then she put her hands on my shoulder and thanked God for giving me a new body. And she asked Him to fill me anew with the Holy Spirit. I was slain by the power of God! I was down almost five minutes. It was so peaceful and again I saw Jesus. It was like floating.

When I got home the first person I called was my minister. It was a Friday evening and he said they were going to a football game but that he would be over in the morning. I said, "You'll be sorry. You'd better come over tonight."

So he and his wife came over. I didn't tell him what it was about, so, when I met them at the door, they stood there speechless. I told them the whole story. Then I gave my testimony in our church.

I have also given it to Baptists, other Methodists, Disciples of Christ, Presbyterians, Latter Day Saints, Assembly of God people, Church of God, Four Square, Community, and Catholics. At first we had a few doubters. One man in our church wasn't ready to fully believe after I gave my testimony. A few weeks later he came around. We had communion and when I went up and knelt at the rail he was right behind me and didn't hear a pop of my joints. I went down so easily on my knees that it convinced him.

Shortly after I was healed I vacationed in Florida. My cousin there took me to church, introduced me, and told about my healing. They asked me to tell about it. I spoke there and somebody was visiting from another church. One thing led to another and I spoke to a string of churches. I went to Puerto Rico to help a former student of mine and her husband who are the directors of a mission school. They asked me to screen their students on a speech and hearing program and to visit them. I went, expecting to be gone about two weeks. I ended up working in their school for eight weeks, five days a week, and speaking in churches on Sundays and on

Wednesday nights.

And, when I've told my story, souls have been saved, and bodies healed. People have been healed of asthma, arthritis, high blood pressure, blindness, deafness, heart conditions and injuries from accidents. God must be given all the praise, all the glory.

Comment

Pearl Bryant's story should encourage older people who find themselves being deprived of the mental abilities and physical strengths of their youth. With God nothing is impossible. Doctor Bryant was pathetically crippled and plagued by excruciating pain. Here again we see a pattern similar to the other miracles in which a friend encouraged her to ask for a healing and brought her to a healing service. Since her healing she has been preaching to others and people in her audiences have been healed. She is a paradigm of the full-healing syndrome.

Interestingly, Doctor Bryant was a devout Christian, yet she never asked God for healing for ten years prior to reading *God Can Do It Again*. The Bible says, "You do not have, because you do not ask" (James 4:2).

It's like having a fat checking account but never writing a check. Surely we need the mercy of God from beginning to end.

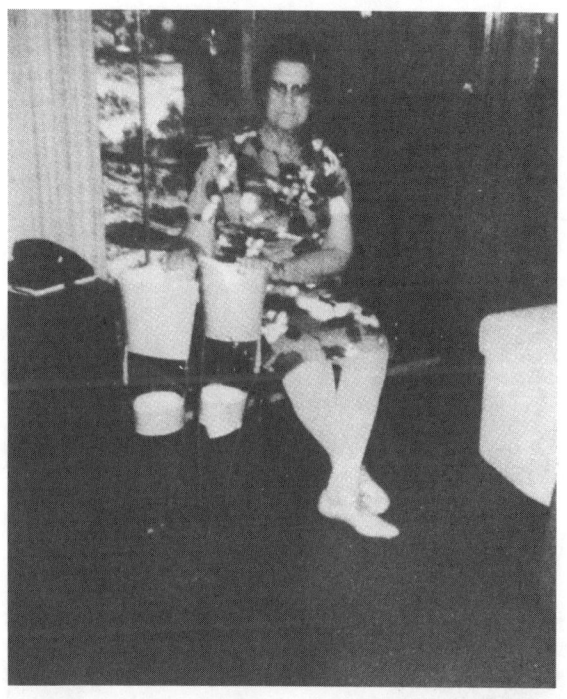

Figure 19: *Doctor Pearl Bryant, after her healing, holding the full-length leg braces which she wore for ten years.*

Figure 20: Mrs. Anne Soults.

Chapter 8

Probable Brain Tumor vs. Infarction of the Brain

Mrs. Anne Soults

On December 23, 1974, while sitting in an attorney's waiting room, Anne Soults noticed she was having difficulty reading her magazine. When she went in to see the lawyer she was unable to express herself adequately. She knew which words she wanted to use, but they would not come when she attempted to speak. And she was having a hard time recalling recent events. This triad of symptoms-dyslexia, aphasia and memory disorder-would gradually increase in severity for the next twenty-seven days.

She was admitted to Valley Presbyterian Hospital, December 26th, for studies. Her first brain scan revealed an abnormality in the left temporal region. She was released December 30th and readmitted January 6, 1975, at which time her studies were repeated. The new brain scan again showed a lesion in the left temporal region. It was larger than on December 27th. (See figures 21 and 22.) During this hospitalization her doctor told her she would need a neurosurgeon to do a biopsy. She was dismissed from the hospital on January 17th.

Dr. William Olson, head of the isotope department at Long Beach Community Hospital reviewed the brain scans on June 2, 1975. He felt that the pattern was consistent with a breakdown in the blood brain barrier in the left temporal-parietal area and that it was most consistent with tumor. He confirmed that the January 6th brain scan showed an increase in the size of the lesion, a pattern still most consistent with tumor.

During her second hospitalization, Anne's physician decided to send her across town to the Los Angeles Good Samaritan Hospital to obtain a computed cranial tomography, commonly called an EMI or computer scan. This sophisticated device helps the clinician differentiate among types of brain lesions. It has rapidly become established as a proven diagnostic technique for the investigation of brain tissue. Its two main advantages are that it requires no surgical invasion of the patient and that it provides a substantially greater amount of data than the traditional brain scan. Its use has greatly enhanced the physician's ability to diagnose lesions and other conditions in the brain and has thus hastened the early treatment of patients with neurological symptoms.

The basic EMI scanner system includes a scanning unit (housing an x ray tube and accurately aligned detectors), an x-ray control unit, computer and magnetic disc unit, a viewing unit, a line printer and a Teletype. It scans a patient's head with a tightly collimated, narrow beam of x-rays. The thickness of the slice under examination is normally thirteen millimeters. A slice thickness of eight millimeters may be selected by the use of additional collimators. The x-ray tube and detectors are mounted diametrically opposite each other on a common frame, so that the detectors receive x-rays after the beam has passed through the patient's head. Two precisely located detectors are used so that two contiguous slices of the head are examined simultaneously. A third detector is used in a reference mode, to measure the intensity of the primary x-ray beam.

Readings from the detector are fed continuously to the system's computer during the scanning procedure. The computer rapidly calculates from this data the 25,600 absorption values of the material within each slice and stores them on the disc, which can hold the results of forty slices. These absorption values are used to build up a picture of each slice in the form of a matrix of 25,600 picture points.

This matrix is displayed as a picture on the cathode ray tube screen of the viewing unit and may be printed out as a permanent record for the patient's chart. The absorption values may also be printed in numerical form by the system's line printer. Physicians-especially neurologists-have hailed this sophisticated (and expensive) unit a truly innovative technique in diagnostic neuroradiology.

Mrs. Soults went for her first EMI scan at the Good Samaritan Hospital on January 10th. Clinicians concluded that she had "low density lesion, left temporo-parietal area with slight increase enhancement following contrast material strongly suggested low grade glioma."

Nine days later she attended a miracle service at the Shrine Auditorium. Following that, on March 10th, Mrs. Soults returned for a repeat EMI scan (computed cranial tomography # 1004). The report came back, "No evidence of any mass lesion on this examination." Dr. William Olson of Long Beach

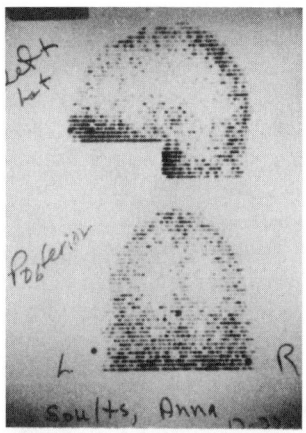

Figure 21: *This brain scan of Anne Soults, obtained December 27, 1974, shows a central density in the lateral projection indicating an abnormality in the left temporal region.*

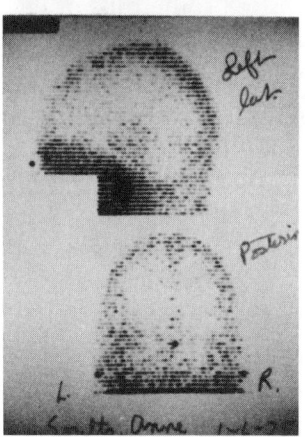

Figure 22: *This repeat brain scan on January 6, 1975, again demonstrates a density in the lateral projection of the scan, indicating an abnormality most consistent with tumor of Anne's left temporal region. This scan also shows that the abnormality had enlarged since December 27th.*

The Miracles

Community Hospital administered a third brain scan to Mrs. Soults later in 1975 and reported, "The isotope cerebral perfusion study and the immediate and delayed static scintiphotos are within normal limits. The abnormality seen on the outside scans of December 27, 1974, and January 6, 1975, are not seen on this study."

The interview with Mrs. Soults follows:

Was the 23rd of December when you first noticed difficulty reading?

Yes. I might have had some hint of it reading the newspaper the Saturday before. It wasn't interesting to me and I was normally an avid newspaper reader. I couldn't find anything I wanted to read, but chalked it up to fatigue. I had had a rough night Friday.

But in the lawyer's office you were reading something and suddenly you realized that you couldn't read it.

That's right, it looked like Arabic! Then I was called into the office and questioned by the two attorneys. I was horrified when I realized I was unable to remember the things they were asking me about. I tried to talk and I couldn't. I looked helplessly first at one man, then the other, then at my husband. I knew something was wrong, but I didn't know what. So I breathed a prayer, "God, help me. I don't want anyone to know that there's something wrong. Just help me." Some words came, I don't remember what they were. They were not the words that I had wanted to say, but the attorneys accepted them.

Were you emotionally upset at the prospect of meeting with the lawyers?

No, I really didn't care all that much about the matter under discussion.

Did you tell your husband about your problem when you went home?

No, but Christmas came and my daughters and their husbands were there with their children. It was then I mentioned casually that I was having difficulty reading and talking. My son-in-law asked me if I had been to see my doctor recently. I told him I had, only two weeks before, and that he had checked my blood pressure and all my medications. I was scheduled to see him again in January. My son-in-law suggested that I might have had a stroke. I checked with my doctor and he put me in the hospital the next day.

You had your first work-up there, a brain scan and an EEG. From their results your doctor must have begun to suspect a brain tumor?

The Miracles

When I was released the first time he said he had given me all the tests he could and would have to put me in the hands of a neurologist. He told me to come back to the hospital in January. I was getting very concerned. I needed someone who could pray for me and with me. My birthday came on January 4th and I was at my daughter's home. We were talking about the implications of my tests and why I would have to go to a neurologist, when my daughter said, "Mom, why don't you read Agnes Stanford's book, *The Healing Light?*" I did and wrote Mrs. Sanford a letter and she replied that she was sorry she couldn't come to pray with me personally, but she gave me the names of four different organizations which had prayer for people with deep needs. I wrote to all four before I re-entered the hospital.

When were you discharged from the first hospitalization in December?

Four days after my admission.

That would be the 30th, and then you went back in on the 6th to the same hospital?

Yes.

Why did you go back in so soon?

Because the doctor told me to. He wanted repeated studies. He had done the EKG, EEG, brain scan, and blood chemistry, but he couldn't go any further than that. He had to have a neurologist. Apparently he saw something in the brain scan that would need further study.

You had your first EMI scan January 10th. Do you know when you went home from that hospitalization?

The 17th of January.

Why were you in so long?

My doctor told me that since I was a schoolteacher, he couldn't release me unless he knew just what was causing my lack of recall and inability to read.

How were your symptoms?

They were worse. My favorite word was thing. I would ask, "What's that thing?" and my daughter would have to supply the word before I could remember it.

That's important because it is typical of a slow-growing tumor. When a person has a stroke it is usually accompanied by aphasia or, worse, paralysis. But generally, in a week or two, he will show some improvement. After a week or two your symptoms, however, were getting worse.

One of the things I couldn't identify was the safety pin. One day the doctor gave me a slip of paper and asked me to write down what he showed me. I recognized it, but I couldn't remember its name.

What other objects did he hold up?

My bedroom slippers. He pointed to a wheelchair, and I called it the thing that ran up and down the halls in the hospital. When I came back from Good Samaritan and the nurse was putting me to bed, she asked how my trip to Good Samaritan Hospital had been. I said it was all right except they took my thing away from me.

"What thing?"

"You know, the things people ride up and down the halls in."

"You mean vacuum sweepers?"

"No, no, those *things!*" It was so frustrating.

"You have a mental block. Why don't you go to sleep? It will come back to you in the morning."

I laid awake half the night drawing the wheels, not knowing what to put on them. Finally I said a prayer and went to sleep. In the morning I remembered it was the wheelchair.

What did your doctor tell you before you went home?

First of all, the doctors told me that I would need surgery because a biopsy was indicated. They told me to get a surgeon right away.

Why didn't they call a neurosurgeon for you?

They wanted to, but I wouldn't let them. I was stubborn. Maybe it was the Lord. I said I would like to talk to two different surgeons. And they recommended one on the staff at the hospital who, they said, was a fine man.

What happened when you left the hospital on January 17th?

I went home weak and still aphasic. I had difficulty reading. My relatives came to visit me on Saturday the 18th; they knew what the doctors had diagnosed. They had lost a very good friend a few weeks prior with a brain tumor. I told them I planned to go to the Kathryn Kuhlman service the next day at the Shrine.

Tell me about that service.

Only my nurse from the hospital, Alice, went with me. Before we left, my husband prayed and, as he did, the thought came to me that you don't go to Kathryn Kuhlman to be prayed for; you go where there is power and the Lord meets you. When I got there I was placed in the lower section where the very sick people were seated.

The Miracles

When the song service began, a man sitting behind me put his hand on my shoulder and prayed in a language I couldn't understand. I began to weep. It was too good to be true. When the miracle service began, I told Alice I had to go up on the stage. The pressure in my head and my headaches were gone.

How long had you had headaches?

They started after they did the angiogram and pneumoencephalogram. When I came out of the EMI scan I was extremely dizzy. They began to disappear during the service, after the man laid his hands on me. I had had difficulty standing in line waiting for the service to begin. I found all sorts of places to sit down, on the curb, on little walls along the front of the Shrine. But when I got up and walked down the aisle to the stage, I felt strong enough to do it without wanting to sit down along the way.

How I got passed the ushers I'll never know, but there was an open path for me to go. When I got up on the stage a man at the microphone announced that I had a brain tumor. Kathryn Kuhlman came over to me. She prayed and then rebuked the brain tumor five times.

Did you go down when she prayed?
I went down once.
What did it feel like?
Like I was floating, I said, Lord, this is the most glorious experience of my life, don't ever let it quit. But they got me on my feet too soon! I went back and walked up that aisle with a renewed strength and vigor. I was praising the Lord for having met me. And yet on the way home the pressures began again. They returned the next day too, so I decided to go to a certain prayer group Monday night. My daughter went with me. It was the first time I had driven my car since Christmas. I was weak, but I drove anyway.

They prayed for me and none of them expressed any doubt that the Lord had healed me completely. I confessed that I had been asking for the Baptism of the Holy Spirit for a long time and asked them to pray for me. They did, but I did not receive a prayer language that night. The next day at home the Lord gave me a prayer language.

What happened after that?
I went to my doctor and told him the Lord had touched me. He looked at me and said, "Anne, I hope so." He gave me a neurological examination and had me

The Miracles

identify everything in his office. I prayed, and was able to do it without any difficulty.

Then, a few days later, early one morning, at five o'clock, I heard a voice from my left shoulder, a loud, shrieking, ugly voice, "Anne, your time is up! " I sat bolt upright in bed, "Who said that?"

My husband awoke and asked what happened. He hadn't heard it and I urged him to go back to sleep. I got up for a drink of hot water and thanked the Lord for letting me sleep until five. (I had not slept well since before Christmas.) Then I rebuked Satan, "This noise was from you. Don't ever do that to me again. In the name of Jesus, leave me!"

A week later I went to a Presbyterian Charismatic meeting in Burbank. My daughter in Pomona thought I might like to go. When I first began having trouble, one of my teacher friends urged me to call for the elders from my church to come and pray for me. I didn't know any elders who could have prayed for me.

Those in the one Presbyterian Church close by me didn't believe in that kind of thing. I had asked God to help me find some who did. So I was glad to discover this Presbyterian meeting in Burbank. While I was there the Holy Spirit helped me and I wept and wept and wept. I couldn't control it. Suddenly I heard a voice. I stopped crying. It was a peaceful, gentlemanly voice, "Anne, you will not die." God knew that I was still filled with the fear of death in my heart.

I went to Kathryn Kuhlman again on February 16th. I went with the same nurse but I didn't sit in the sick section, I was in the balcony. The man sitting next to me asked if I was sick.

"Yes, I think so."

"Do you have cancer?"

"I don't think so. If I do, it's in the brain where I have a tumor."

"Oh, I guess I added to what the Lord was telling me. You see, this has never happened to me before, but the Lord told me that you have a stomach condition and a tumor, and that I should tell you that everything will be all right, that the Lord has taken care of it."

That really thrilled me and then, a little later, an usher came over to me. I told him my story and he took me to a counselor named Marion. When she heard my story she told me I should tell it to the whole Shrine audience as soon as I had a clear brain scan. On March

10th the EMI scan gave no evidence of a tumor, and I spoke at the Shrine in April.

Comment

This lady's brain abnormality was well documented by the standard diagnostic techniques and she was seen by many specialists. Electroencephalographic study (brain wave pattern) was performed in each of her hospitalizations. The repeat study dated January 6th reported "abnormal EEG, suggesting left temporal pathology. There is no significant change since 12/27/74."

The discharge summary dictated by her physician on January 17th, included the following information:

> *Repeat encephalogram again showed changes in the left temporal area and repeat brain scan still showed a suggestive lesion in the left temporal area. Spinal fluid examination revealed three cells, all lymphocytes, protein 29 mg %. Patient was sent on 1/10/75 to Good Samaritan Hospital for EMI scan performed which was not diagnostic but somewhat suggestive of a tumor in the left posterior temporal area.*
>
> *On 1/14 bilateral carotid angiograms showed only faint suggestion of a left-to-*

right shift of the anterior cerebral arteries, otherwise no definite abnormality. Pneumoencephalogram showed no definite abnormality. It was felt that neurosurgical consultation should be performed. She was seen by Dr. ————— who, after reviewing all her tests, felt the possibility of a very early tumor the most likely diagnosis.

The clinical impression was that of brain tumor and during a period of medical observation her symptoms suddenly and completely disappeared following a visit to the Shrine service.

While seated at the Shrine Auditorium, before the service began, an unknown Christian, seated behind Mrs. Soults, placed his hands on her shoulders and prayed for her. Following this prayer her symptoms cleared completely. Subsequent diagnostic studies showed clearing of the abnormality which had previously been evident on her electroencephalogram (brain wave pattern), brain scan and EMI scan (computed cranial tomography).

Mrs. Soults was also changed spiritually. She received gifts of the Spirit, including a prayer language, and has been given a new ministry of sharing her testimony with others.

Her family members remark how different she was following her healing. Her husband,

The Miracles

who is a Presbyterian minister, said that it was as if she had been born again. Her daughter said that she had a song in her voice. Mrs. Soults herself reports that God told her she had to forgive several people before her ministry could continue. She did, and her ministry has continued. Mrs. Soults frequently shares her testimony. She has returned to the classroom where she is a popular teacher.

Figure 23: *Mr. Paul W. Trousdale*

Chapter 9

Massive GI Hemorrhage with Shock, Instantaneously Healed

Paul Whitney Trousdale

*W*HEN PAUL TROUSDALE GAVE THE COMmencement address at Pepperdine University June 13, 1975, newspapers across the country and in Honolulu took note of it. More than 25,000 quality homes and many commercial complexes in California and Hawaii bear the stamp of Paul Trousdale. This prominent builder and civic leader has gained a reputation for superior work. He was chairman of Trousdale Construction Company, which he established in 1946, until 1969, when Leer-Siegler Inc. bought him out and he became a consultant for them. Soon after that he was elected to the Leer-Siegler board of directors.

Among his California projects are the Trousdale Estates in Beverly Hills, the Baldwin Hills subdivision, a 200-acre industrial park in San Diego and the Mills Estate in Burlingame and Milbray. His company also built and operates the International Marketplace in Waikiki, Honolulu. Among other projects he has built and sold are the Tahquitz River Estates in Palm Springs and the ten thousand acre Kaneohe Ranch in Oahu, Hawaii.

A graduate of the University of Southern California, Mr. Trousdale is a member of the board of regents of St. John's Hospital in Santa Monica, trustee of the Eisenhower Medical Center in Palm Springs, and a member of the associates of the University Southern California, California Institute of Technology and University of Hawaii. He also serves as a trustee of Webb School a trustee of USC and, since his healing, as a member of the boar Christ Church in Los Angeles.

I obtained copies of Mr. Trousdale's medical records from John's Hospital in Santa Monica. He was admitted there December 12, 1973, and dismissed January 4, 1974. He was suffering from gastrointestinal hemorrhaging which required many blood transfusions during the first few days of his hospitalization. The bleeding and blood transfusions continued until his instantaneous healing. He was markedly anemic upon admission with a hemoglobin of 8.4 (normal 14-17.0) recorded on December 27, 1973. Thereafter, the hemoglobin ranged from 8.4 to 9.8 in spite of repeated blood transfusions. After his healing, the hemoglobin gradually rose to essentially normal values by the time he left the hospital.

Mr. Trousdale today is a handsome man with a large athletic build. He appears considerably younger than his sixty-one years. In spite of his history of vigorous health, on Christmas Day, 19 he fainted for the first time in his life. He fainted twice more during the night and was taken by ambulance to St. John's Hospital in Santa Monica. There physicians quickly realized he had lost a great deal of blood internally and started blood transfusions.

After four days of this conservative therapy he was still bleeding continuously. His doctors ruled out diagnostic x-rays under the circumstances and were planning exploratory surgery to find source of the bleeding. During the night of December 28th, Trousdale seemed to have suddenly lost blood pressure, broke in a profuse sweat (diaphoresis), and, possibly, lost consciousness.

When he opened his eyes the following morning he found his wife had called the

The Miracles

Reverend John Hinkle to his bedside. They prayed and a miracle of healing occurred. Mr. Trousdale had been raised, baptized and confirmed in the Episcopal Church. However, during the preceding six months he and Mrs. Trousdale had been attending services conducted by John Hinkle at Christ Church in Los Angeles. Hinkle had taught them that the Lord Jesus Christ, through the Holy Spirit, appears and touches the lives of some of us in miraculous ways.

Hinkle told Trousdale that Jesus and the Holy Spirit had healed the internal bleeding and that no tumor, ulcer, tear, or scar would ever be found, because the Lord had completely healed him. Paul closed his eyes and repeated a prayer after the minister. As he did he saw Pastor Hinkle on the right side of the bed praying and Jesus on the left side. A warmness ran through his body and he had a sense of well-being as never before. He extended his hand toward Jesus and felt a warm, firm handclasp in return.

Paul immediately wanted to go home. His physicians wisely insisted that he remain for diagnostic studies, which, as Pastor Hinkle predicted, were all negative, revealing no obvious source for the massive bleeding which had necessitated the transfusions. On December 31st, a barium study of the upper gastrointestinal tract with small bowel follow-through was entirely normal.

The doctors were at a loss to account for the patient's bleeding. They could see no abnormality at all of the esophagus, stomach, duodenum or small bowel. On January 3rd, a barium enema showed some diverticulosis of the sigmoid colon (a common finding in Americans), but no other significant abnormality and no source of bleeding.

Following his release from the hospital, Mr. Trousdale has remained healthy, and subsequent examinations have not revealed any abnormality. He has resumed his active professional life but he is a changed man spiritually. Following is the interview I conducted in his office on November 6, 1975:

What happened before you went to the hospital on December 26th?
Around noon on Christmas Day, I fainted. I got up a couple times during the night and fainted again. So we called the doctor who sent me to the hospital and took my blood count, which was very low. They started giving me blood transfusions. I was in the hospital about four days taking transfusions. A surgeon and everybody else were trying to find out where the blood was coming from and how to get it stopped.

The Miracles

Had you not been bothered by peptic ulcers before? Did this come as a total surprise?

No, I hadn't. It was totally unexpected.

I gather that at one point, in spite of blood transfusions, your condition deteriorated and you went into shock, with a low blood pressure?

That's right. I had been taking a transfusion, the needle was still in my arm when I felt deathly cold, began perspiring profusely and felt like I was passing out.

Did you lose consciousness?

Yes. I rang the bell for the nurse before I went out. Some doctors came in and I recovered from that episode.

When was it that Pastor John Hinkle came on the scene?

I think he came early the next morning with my wife. They came in and talked a few minutes. Then my wife left John and me alone in the room. John said, "I feel the presence of the Lord and the Holy Spirit in your room. You are going to be completely healed at this moment and there will be no sign of ulcer or anything else afterward." I was still bleeding. I had been bleeding that morning...

How do you know?

Evidence from the jet-black stool. And I was quite weak. I thought I'd pass out again and was about as low physically as I could get. John asked me to repeat a prayer with him. I closed my eyes and felt the presence of the Lord in the room. I clearly saw Christ standing there and I was startled by it. I reached out my left hand. John was on my right. Christ took my hand and I felt the cold chill leave. I felt that the bleeding stopped at that moment. I was jubilant and told everybody who came into the room that I believed I was okay.

Weren't you religious prior to this?

No. We'd say our prayers every night and probably went to church two or three times a year. My wife started going to John Hinkle's church and I went with her. Hinkle's message appealed to me. We started going fairly regularly for about six months. Then this happened.

Do you recall the prayer John Hinkle asked you to repeat after him?

It was a very positive prayer. I accepted the healing and turned over my problem to God. It was along those lines. I've heard him use it since then.

Can you describe how Christ appeared in the vision?

He appeared in white robes, like the

traditional paintings of Christ.

Was there any radiance around His face?

Yes.

You reached out your hand and He grabbed it?

In that brief span I was completely cured. A warm feeling flowed through my body. As a matter of fact I said to John, "I'm all cured."

This was a totally new experience for you?

Yes, I always believed in Christ, but if someone had told me about such an experience prior to this, I would have thought it was nice, but I would have to have seen it to believe it. I saw and I believed.

After the healing I wanted to go home that very day. I told the doctors the bleeding stopped and to let me out! They said no. Since I had never been able to have any taken because I was bleeding, they wanted to get some x-rays and find out what caused the bleeding.

Did they ever find out?

No, all the studies were negative. They gave me all of them, the upper and lower, the barium, and everything they could think of.

And you were feeling well all this time?

I felt perfect.

Are you different since that experience?

Yes. Before we started going to Christ Church, my wife and I were having some difficulties and I was drinking quite a bit. After this incident of my healing, I stopped all that. We go to church and pray regularly. I got on the board of the church, and my wife goes to the Bible class during the week. I am a one-hundred-percent believer now and, if I have any business or other problems, I turn it over to Christ and depend on Him to show me what to do or work it out some other way.

Have you had any interesting experiences since your healing?

A very wealthy and self-sufficient lady called my wife, which she had never done before, and asked if she could get some help for her daughter who was ill with a strange malady. We got John Hinkle to talk to her and we prayed for her daughter. Her condition was unusual; I really don't know the facts. After that they took her out of St. John's and flew her to the Mayo Clinic. But they couldn't find anything wrong with her! I think our prayers were really helping.

Comments

The illness which threatened Paul Trousdale's life was of relatively short duration. It is well documented by medical records and involves a prominent businessman.

Once again, other Christians - his wife, Jean, and Pastor John Hinkle -prayed with Paul Trousdale at the time of his healing. Not only was he instantaneously healed, with a feeling of warmth and restoration of vitality, but he was changed spiritually as well.

A special element of mystery marks this story. That is the complete disappearance of any indication of what might have caused Paul's massive hemorrhaging. Neither his history nor diagnostic tests give the slightest hint. Any opinion would be, at best, an educated guess.

Chapter 10

Osteoporosis of the Entire Spine with Intractable Pain Requiring Bilateral Cordotomies

Delores Winder

DELORES WINDER WAS A DEVOUT PRESBYterian and it was with great reluctance that she contemplated attending a Methodist convention on the Holy Spirit scheduled for August 30, 1975. Kathryn Kuhlman, whom she had never watched on television because she didn't believe in that kind of healing, was going to be speaking. But a friend questioned her, "What if you're keeping a door closed?" It was only then that she prayed about it and decided she should go.

Miss Kuhlman spoke of the Holy Spirit's presence and ability to do anything. Then

The Miracles

she prayed and Delores realized that her legs were on fire. The sensation startled her because her bilateral cordotomies, which had been done to relieve severe pain in her spine and lower extremities, had left her without any feeling in her legs. But she put it out of her mind.

When Miss Kuhlman prayed with someone up on the stage and the person fell to the floor, Delores' misgivings were confirmed. The service had been so beautiful, why, she wondered, did Miss Kuhlman have to spoil it with such theatrical demonstrations. She turned to her friend, "Let's go." Before her friend could answer, a stranger asked Delores why she wore a neck brace. "I have a bad neck."

"Something is happening, isn't it?"

"Well, my legs are burning like crazy."

"Do you want to talk more about it?"

"Yes, outside."

So he helped Delores up and they started out of the building. He asked about her surgeries and she mentioned casually that she had had four spinal fusions and two cordotomies. She expected him to ask her what a cordotomy was. Instead he remarked, "And your legs are burning. Isn't that strange?"

When they got to the rear of the auditorium he told Delores she could take off her cast if she wanted to. Delores had worn a body cast for fourteen years. She started to object but she had a feeling he knew something she didn't. She accepted his advice and he escorted her back into the auditorium whereupon Miss Kuhlman asked them to come up on the stage. It was then that she learned who this mysterious stranger was: Dr. Richard O'Wellen of Johns Hopkins Medical School, a loyal friend and supporter of Miss Kuhlman.

I will let Delores take up the story at this point:

> At no time did I believe this was possible. Yet I had no pain. I was walking without my cast. I'd even gotten rid of my headache and I could feel my legs. It was utterly fantastic to me. My mind was reeling and I was not certain of anything. My son had said before I left that I would be healed. But I had ruled out even the possibility of such a thing.
>
> When Miss Kuhlman touched me I was sure I would not go down, but I did. Two weeks later in Oklahoma City she touched me again and I felt as if plugs were pulled from the bottom of my feet and everything drained out of me. It was like being wrapped in the arms of a great love. My husband and son were aware of this too. On the way home,

unintelligible words were running through my mind. When I picked up my Bible after this it was like I had never read it before. I began to know things I had no way of knowing. I got feelings about people or something I ought to do that made no sense, yet, when I did what those feelings suggested, I soon discovered the reason.

I am now speaking regularly in churches and never know what I'm going to say-I just pray. He speaks the words and, so far, it has gone well. I still do not like the publicity, but a wise person told me, "You're the package God put a miracle in and people need to see the package."

Mrs. Winder's medical history in her own testimony follows:

Between January 1957, and August 1972, I had four back fusions (lower lumbar), another operation to remove spurs from the fusion, and two cordotomies. The first fusion was done to correct three deformed vertebrae and scoliosis. It held three years, and then broke. I returned to the same surgeon and had the second fusion. It was not long before I had further trouble. In 1964 I had to have spikes removed. Then I spent much

Figure 24: *Delores Winder holding the cast she had worn for the last eighteen months prior to her healing. She had worn out seven casts in the preceding fourteen years. In her right hand is her neck brace.*

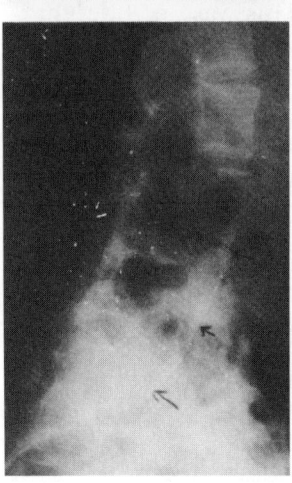

Figure 25: *This x-ray of Delores Winder's lumbar spine was obtained January 15, 1975. The radiologist interpreted it to show moderate osteoporosis (that is, thinning of the amount of calcium and protein in the bones). The arrows in the front or anterior part of the lumbar spine show disc disease and the sites of the anterior interbody fusion, that is, the fusion of the anterior or front part of the lumbar spine.*

time in bed and in a plaster-of-Paris cast. My family doctor was giving me novocaine injections in the spine along with pain medication. In 1966 I was hospitalized. After x-rays and consultation with an internal medicine specialist they diagnosed my problem as pseudoarthrosis and osteoporosis.

The doctor decided to do a frontal fusion (a frontal fusion approaches the spinal column from the front through the abdomen rather than from the back) hoping there would be less pressure and it would hold. It held about eighteen months. Then they did the first percutaneous cordotomy. This was on the right side and was done to the neck level. After a time the fusion broke again and they did the fourth fusion.

Then, in 1972, I had the second cordotomy (for the opposite side of the body). This one could only be taken to a little above waist level because my lungs were not strong enough to take it higher. I still had intense pain above that level and, in 1973, I fell. That started the trouble in my neck and left shoulder and I had to go into a Queen Anne collar. I had very bad headaches and could not turn my head. My shoulder hurt so much that when the doctor examined me, he could not put much pressure on it until after my healing.

I was on pain medication, tranquilizers and at least six other medications all the time. There were complications too. I was also taking medicines for kidney, stomach, low blood pressure, and bowel conditions. In addition, I had a herniated esophagus. After my fall in 1973, they could not stabilize my general health.

In January 1975, the neurosurgeon did another myelogram and told me nothing more could be done, but that I would live longer by going to bed and staying still. Before this I was only allowed out of bed three hours a day, one hour at a time. After much prayer, my husband and I decided I should continue to be up as much as I could manage. I was getting weaker all the time, but did not want my fourteen-year-old son to remember me in a hospital bed.

Medical Documentation

I have medical records on this lady an inch thick. They document her story and I will only briefly summarize them here. Cordotomies are normally reserved for patients with cancer and extreme pain. This alone should illustrate that she does not exaggerate the severity of her condition.

The Miracles

In summary:

1) Lumbar spine fusion, 1957, with bone grafts from tibia. Spinal fusion of 3rd, 4th and 5th lumbar vertebrae.
2) Repeat spinal fusion with bone graft from tibia, 1961, due to trauma when the patient broke the first graft.
3) In 1965 the patient had excision of spinous processes thought to be contributing to pain. The graft was reported to be solid at this time.
4) In 1967 the patient had anterior interbody fusion, L-3-4, L-4-5, L-5-S-1.
5) In 1968 a percutaneous cordotomy was performed after severe pain had continued. This was done in Dallas, Texas, at Parkland Memorial Hospital for relief of right-side pain. The physicians regarded it as very successful.
6) In 1970 the patient underwent her fourth fusion of the lumbar spine because of recurrence of pain. Patient continued to have pain. She was fitted with two molded plastic body casts and took several Talwin tablets per day and occasionally had injections of Talwin for relief of pain.
7) August, 1972, the patient underwent a second percutaneous cordotomy down at level C-6 and C-7 with good

relief of her pain. This was done to relieve the pain on the left side of the body and removed all sensation on the left up to the waist level. This was done at Fort Worth, Texas.

Unfortunately, the patient had recurrent pain in other parts of her body even after the cordotomies and she was left with altered and decreased sensation in the lower extremities. She had a gradual downhill course, as described in her testimony, up to the time of her healing. Since that time she has been leading a completely normal life without medication, braces or body cast. The medical diagnoses in this case include:

1) Extensive osteoporosis of the spine.
2) Pseudoarthrosis of the spine.
3) Severe intractable pain requiring bilateral percutaneous cordotomy for relief.
4) Status post-operative laminectomy and fusion x4.
5) Trauma to the right shoulder and neck with pain.

The medical records indicate that in spite of bilateral cordotomies, an extreme procedure, the patient gradually had a recurrence of pain in the low back, neck and shoulders

The Miracles

requiring injections for local relief of pain. The records indicate that this discomfort was becoming progressively worse and that it was unrelated to trauma or over activity.

According to medical records dated May 22, 1974, she was taking Percodan, or Phenergan, and Talwin. She was losing weight, getting around poorly, and had to be helped on and off the table. There were restricted movements of her lower back with localized discomfort.

The last note in the medical records before her healing is dated August 6, 1975. Her physician remarked that she did not look good; she felt poorly, was depressed with back discomfort at the level of D-6-7. Her nails were cracking and she also had an ulcerated area about her lower back where the brace irritated the skin.

The last notation on her chart was made, after her healing, on September 3, 1975. The physician commented that the patient had had some sort of "faith healing" experience and had apparently "gotten an excellent result physically and ... emotionally.... Her girdle ... does not fit her because she stands up so much straighter. " He thought the feeling in her feet wasn't quite normal, but that her back was more mobile, her neck and shoulders better, and her leg signs negative.

Mrs. Winder acknowledged that following her healing on August 30, 1975, she did have a slight residual numbness in the front part of the hip areas and burning in the posterior hip areas. However, after Miss Kuhlman prayed for her and she fell to the floor, all feeling became normal and she has since been free of pain.

To relieve, or at least control the severe and disabling pain which this patient experienced over a period of many years, physicians elected to employ a surgical oblative technique known as percutaneous cordotomy. Since this is an unusual technique of which the reader may not be aware, a short discussion of cordotomy follows.

Spinal Cordotomy for Relief of Intractable and Disabling-Pain

Spinal cordotomy (literally, cutting the spinal cord) is particularly useful for the relief of widespread pain in the trunk and extremities. It is especially helpful when the pain originates from the thoracic or abdominal regions. Surgeons cut the cord opposite the side of the pain in the anterolateral quadrant of the spinal cord at least six cord segments above the origin of the pain.

The analgesia (relief of pain) resulting from a cordotomy covers the opposite half of the body beginning several segments below the point at which the cord is cut. For complete relief of pain the entire lateral spinothalmic tract must be cut through. Anything less might allow pain to persist. Delores Winder underwent percutaneous cervical cordotomy. This means that, instead of opening her surgically, the doctors inserted a needle through the skin into the spinal cord in order to interrupt the spinothalmic pathways. This technique was introduced by Mullan in 1963 and has proven useful in patients who could not withstand the rigors of conventional surgery on the spinal cord.

Since this technique does not permit the surgeon to see what he is doing, x-ray is used to guide a coagulating needle into the anterolateral quadrant of the spinal cord, usually between the first and second cervical vertebrae. Electrical stimulation can be used to test the location of the needle tip within the spinal cord.

The lateral spinothalamic tract can be coagulated by means of a high frequency electrical current. It remains, however, a blind operation and the surgeon must exercise care not to misplace the lesion and cause additional neurologic deficit, such as paralysis. One risk of the percutaneous technique is that the high cervical cord lesions may interfere with breathing. A percutaneous cordotomy is most commonly applied to poor risk patients with short life expectancy.

Anatomic Considerations

The cordotomy is based on precise anatomic and physiological knowledge. The fibers which carry pain to the cerebrum enter the spinal cord, ascend a few segments, cross the midline, and form the antero-lateral tract. Because about ninety percent of pain fibers cross, a cordotomy performed on one side of the spinal cord relieves pain on the opposite side of the body.

The anterolateral spinothalamic) tract tends to be segmented with the sacral fibers peripherally near the equator while the thoracic and cervical fibers lie more anteriorly and medially. The dentate ligament, which supports the spinal cord, stands between the motor corticospinal tract posteriorly (behind) and the sensory anterolateral tract anteriorly (in front). Thus, if we know the position of the dentate ligament, we can also ascertain the position of the anterolateral tract.

Technique of Percutaneous Cervical Cordotomy

The patient is sedated and lies face down with his or her head fixed in a suitable holder. A spinal needle is inserted between the first and second cervical vertebra below the mastoid process under local anesthesia and the cerebrospinal fluid obtained. An emulsion of iophendylate is injected. This settles on the dentate ligament, which appears as a line across the x-ray film. The anterior border of the cord is usually apparent too. The spinal needle tip is then aimed two millimeters in front of the dentate ligament by raising the hub with an elevator, in other words it points at the anterolateral tract. The depth of penetration is checked by an anterolateral film.

Stimulation Studies and Coagulation

Following this, stimulation studies are carried out with a suitable electric current. If the electrode is correctly positioned in the anterolateral tract, stimulation will produce parasthesias (pins and needles sensation) on the opposite side of the body, which the patient can report. If the electrode is incorrectly situated in the motor tract, it will cause movement of the body on the same side. If the electrode is situated in the anterior horn cells, then movement of the neck muscles on the same side will occur.

When the electrode is in the correct position, the anterolateral (spinothalamic) tract is coagulated. A radio-frequency current produces a heat lesion. Each lesion generator has to be standardized to produce a lesion of about twenty square millimeters in about thirty seconds.

During and between coagulation, physicians check the patient's motor power. If they detect the slightest suggestion of motor weakness, the procedure is stopped. Also, between coagulations, they check the reduction of pain on the opposite side of the body by pin-prick testing.

In summary, percutaneous cervical cordotomy is a technique applied for pain relief in patients with incapacitating and disabling pain. It is most commonly applied to terminal cancer patients, although occasionally to others, like Delores Winder, who suffer chronic, severe and disabling pain.

Comments

Mrs. Delores Winder presents us with an unusual case of severe, chronic, disabling pain secondary to osteoporosis, which her physicians tried to relieve by five different spine operations. In desperation they resorted to a bilateral percutaneous cordotomy.

This patient's symptoms had begun early in 1957. After 1962, she had worn a full-body cast or brace of some sort. Most of the time it was a full-body cast, although at the time of her healing she was in a lightweight, full-body plastic shell.

Although she did not believe in instant miraculous healing, she attended a lecture by Miss Kuhlman in Dallas on August 30, 1975.

The Miracles

She was miraculously healed beginning with a sensation of heat in both lower extremities from the thighs down.

She has been restored to full health, wears no brace or support, takes no medication, and has completely normal sensations in the lower extremities. This is unusual because the spinothalamic nerve tracts in the spinal cord had been interrupted on both sides and, in such cases, the ensuing numbness is usually permanent.

Delores doesn't enjoy being before the public - as she often has been since her healing - but she obediently proclaims the miracle-working power of God as she learns to walk in the Spirit.

* Dr. Anselmo Pineda, M.D., F.A.C.S., was kind enough to review this chapter with special attention to the section dealing with spinal cordotomy for control of pain. Dr. Pineda is a Diplomate of the American Board of Neurosurgery and is widely regarded as an authority in the field of control of pain problems by the use of various neurosurgical techniques, including the implantation of neuropacemakers.

Chapter 11

A Physician's Conclusions

*T*HE PEOPLE IN THIS BOOK WERE HEALED BY the power of the Holy Spirit. Meeting the Holy Spirit is simple. We need only ask our heavenly Father:

> *If you then, who are evil, know how to give good gifts to your children, how much more will the heavenly Father give the Holy Spirit to those who ask Him!* (Luke 11: 13)

I have known people who have done this at home or while driving. Most, however, have received the Baptism of the Holy Spirit after prayer with other Christians. Jesus Christ is the one who baptizes us with the Holy Spirit, as John the Baptist stated in Matthew 3:11:

The Miracles

> *I baptize you with water for repentance, but he who is coming after me is mightier than I, whose sandals I am not worthy to carry; he will baptize you with the Holy Spirit and with fire.*

The miraculous ministry of Jesus did not begin until the Holy Spirit came upon Him:

> *And when Jesus was baptized, he went up immediately from the water, and behold, the heavens were opened and he saw the Spirit of God descending like a dove, and alighting on him.* (Matthew 3:16)

Jesus was then led by the Spirit into the wilderness to be tempted by the devil. The work of the Holy Spirit will be opposed by the enemy.

Paul received the Holy Spirit at the same time his sight was restored (Acts 9:17). Later, when Paul came to Ephesus, he found some disciples and asked them if they had received the Holy Spirit since they had believed. They told him that they had never even heard that there was a Holy Spirit (Acts 19:2). When Paul laid his hands upon them, the Holy Spirit came on them; and they spoke with tongues and prophesied (Acts 19:6).

The Holy Spirit is a person whom we must meet and experience. He not only empowered the apostles but spoke with them and guided their steps. He will speak to us and guide us today as He did in their day.

This Holy Spirit is as active (if not more so) today as He was in apostolic times. Because the Holy Spirit spoke to Herman Rosenberger, he decided to rely only on Jesus Christ to heal Marie. I am glad to be a physician and I believe God uses medical science to benefit humanity. But there are all too many cases for which medical science does not have the answer. Only those who are totally blinded by arrogant self-assurance fail to recognize our helplessness as humans and our utter need of Jesus. This is the day of the ministry of the Holy Spirit.

The Role of the Individual in Healing

We are responsible for one another. God entrusts us with His concern and love for people who have problems, whether mental, physical or spiritual. He assigns us to certain people, and if we do not respond obediently, we will be the cause of suffering and even death.

Looking at the cases in this book, we learn that God regularly works through individuals. If those individuals had not done what they thought God told them to do, some and

The Miracles

maybe all of the miracles recorded in this book might not have happened. Some of the individuals would probably be dead today.

Helen Smith, a lady in her seventh decade of life, had not seen Marion Burgio for eleven years. But, at the prompting of the Holy Spirit, Helen went to the hospital and told her old friend that she was going to be healed. Marion was at a low ebb after twelve years of multiple sclerosis. She suffered permanent muscular weakness, deformity, partial blindness, deafness, and loss of bowel and bladder control.

Helen had nothing to encourage her except the unseen presence of God, yet, by His grace, she persisted with Marion and God allowed her to see the fruit of her obedience. I firmly believe that if Helen had not obeyed and if Marion had not gone to the healing service, she would still be an invalid in a wheelchair today, or perhaps worse.

There are times when a person is too ill or near death to pray for himself. Herman Rosenberger prayed for his wife, Marie, when she was near death. Herman himself thought Marie was going to die. His faith was, in his own words, zero. Then he ceased to be the Reverend Mr. Rosenberger, he ceased to be the Dean of Students of LIFE Bible College. He became a child and besought the mercy of his heavenly Father. In his emptiness and lowliness God met him and healed his wife.

Lisa Larios and her mother were encouraged by a friend, Bill Truit, to go to the Kathryn Kuhlman service. Bill's mother had prophesied that Lisa would be healed and, during the week preceding their visit to the service, Bill fasted and prayed for Lisa's healing. And his prayers were answered that Sunday at the Shrine Auditorium. What would have happened to Lisa had their friend Bill refused the burden of responsibility for this girl?

Shortly before the service began, Mrs. Anne Soults took her seat in the Shrine Auditorium. A man seated behind her placed his hands on her shoulders and said, "Sister, God has told me to pray for you." As he prayed, the tears started flooding out of Anne's eyes and, when he finished, he said, "Sister, you have been healed." Following that, all of Anne's symptoms of aphasia, dyslexia and memory disorder completely disappeared, never to return again.

The inescapable conclusion is that God uses us to help others. There are times when He gives us a specific burden for another individual and, if we do not obey that call, the task may possibly never be done. If Herman Rosenberger had not prayed as he did on that specific night for his wife, Marie, she probably would not be alive on this earth today.

The Miracles

I had a dream one night about the Rosenberger healing. It was before I met them. In this dream I was told that Marie Rosenberger was not healed in the Shrine Auditorium. And she was healed in one hour. I didn't know what to make of this information until I sat down with Herman and Marie and heard their testimony.

You Have a Right to be Happy

Every prayer we utter is answered if we allow it to be answered. Many of us do not realize that, in some prayers, our own cooperation is involved in the answer. In May 1975, Miss Kuhlman held a healing service at the North Hollywood Assembly of God Church. A stream of people came forward claiming to have been delivered from a variety of medical conditions.

Toward the end of the service Miss Kuhlman announced, "Someone has been healed of a spinal condition, but has not claimed the healing. This individual should take off his back brace, stand up, claim his healing, and come forward. If this individual does not do so and leaves this auditorium without claiming his healing, he will lose it."

I pondered the significance of her assertion. I was in the midst of my research for this book. I was thoroughly convinced of the authenticity of these miracles, and their impact on the lives of those who experienced them. That a person might have his twisted and tormented body touched by a miracle, only to leave and lose it, utterly astonished me. Yet many people are apparently so engrossed in their own *self-image*, as either depressed or chronically ill, that when God comes upon them, they turn and walk away.

If we are prone to self-pity firmly enough we can perhaps even turn down our own healing. Sometimes part of our healing is up to us. Sometimes God requires us to stand up and claim our healing. Sometimes He insists that we humble ourselves by going to a Kathryn Kuhlman meeting. Sometimes we must abandon medical treatments. Whatever, the key is trusting obedience to God's true guidance.

A very dear friend of mine has been chronically depressed during much of her adult life. She has seen psychiatrists from one end of the country to the other. She has had electro-shock therapy and taken virtually all of the drugs modem psychiatry has to offer. Recently her depression started to lift, due to the power of God. I believe she could have been instantly healed years ago if she had asked God for help, and then accepted her healing through His power.

In my experience, people who have received a miracle of physical healing agree

The Miracles

that they also were recipients of God's further grace of spiritual healing-many of them speak, in fact, of being born again-and that if they had to give up one of their hearings, the physical or the spiritual, they would always hold on to the spiritual and give up the physical, if that were required.

There is no doubt that we are surrounded by the invisible kingdom of God. To see it we must be born anew by the Spirit of God. This rebirth is always more important than physical healing. That is because our spirits ultimately leave our bodies. Death comes to every man, no matter how good his health. After our spiritual rebirth, we may face death with assurance that our lives are hid with Christ in God-that death has no final power over us.

Dr. Elisabeth Kubler-Ross, a noted Chicago psychiatrist, has accumulated some fascinating information about the dying experience. Over many years she has studied people who have been clinically dead and then resuscitated by medical means. The medical reports of postmortem spiritual experiences by these individuals are so consistent that she has proven to her satisfaction that life after death does occur and, furthermore, that the dying experience is pleasant.

Many of the people she interviewed reported that they were disappointed to return to life from the experience they were enjoying on the other side of this existence. She explains, "We have found some fabulous common denominators which you can't deny."* Most of those she interviewed said they recalled floating a few feet above their bodies, watching the resuscitation efforts. They could accurately recall the scene, the details of what was said, and the comings and goings of rescuers. "They have a fabulous feeling of peace and wholeness," Ross reported. "People who are blind can see, paraplegics have legs that they can move. They have no pain, no fear, no anxiety." Almost all of them reported that they were greeted by someone who had died before them. "It is a good feeling to be able to say after many years that people really don't die. Death is simply a shedding of the physical body."

Of course, the Bible is much more explicit about the nature of life beyond the grave. Its picture is not so consistently pleasant, but those who have embraced Christ as Lord are promised a place in His Father's house. We do live beyond physical death and those who have salvation will be with Jesus.

Resurrections have been reported throughout history. Some have involved medical figures-especially in the twentieth century-and some religious figures. When all is said and done, death comes ultimately to everyone.

The important thing to be sure of when it does come is that we will enter heaven by the grace of Jesus Christ.

Come Holy Spirit

And now we are at the end-or is it a new beginning? Certainly each of the ten formerly very sick people in this book found a new beginning in their lives. Their hearings were only signals of that beginning. The substance, in each case, was Jesus Christ. He alone can bestow new birth upon men and women.

Thus, in Christ, each of these miracles is not merely an isolated event but participates in the kingdom of God. Miracles gain transcendent meaning when they point to the mercy of the Lord Jesus and serve to substantiate His claim to be the Messiah of Israel, the Son of God. That, after we have examined all the records and checked all the facts, is *the real meaning of the miracles!*

*Kubler-Ross, Elisabeth, *Death, The Final Stage of Growth*, Prentice-Hall, New Jersey, 1975. Dr. Ross was kind enough to read the report of her work given in the chapter and approves of its accuracy.

Appendix

Curriculum Vitae

Herman Richard Casdorph, M.D., Ph.D.

Date of Birth: November 8, 1928; Charleston, West Virginia

Pre-Medical Education
West Virginia University, Morgantown, 1946-1949. A.B. Degree with High Honors, 1949.

Medical School
Indiana University Medical School, 1949-1953. M.D. Degree, June 15, 1953.

Postgraduate Training
Internship, Rotating, 1953-1954, Indiana University Medical Center, Indianapolis.

Fellowship in Internal Medicine, Mayo Foundation, 1954-1955 and 1957-1960, Rochester, Minnesota.

Assistant to Staff in Cardiovascular Diseases, Mayo Clinic, 1960-1961.

Ph.D. Degree in Medicine, University of Minnesota, December 14, 1961.

Special Courses

School of Aviation Medicine, Air University, United States Air Force, October-December, 1955.

Recipient of Research Fellowship by National Institutes of Health for twelve months, 1959-1960 (while at Mayo Foundation, Rochester, Minnesota). Postdoctoral Fellowship.

Special Course in Radioisotopes for licensure at Mayo Clinic, 1959.

Military Service

Captain, United States Air Force Medical Corps., Flight Surgeon, 1611th USAF Disp., McGuire Air Force Base, New Jersey, April, 1955-September, 1957.

Certification and Licensure

Physician's License, State of Indiana, June 30, 1954.

Physician's License, State of Minnesota, February 14, 1958.

Physician's and Surgeon's Certificate, State of California, October 5, 1961.

Diplomate of American Board of Internal Medicine, September 13, 1962.

Awards and Honors

Phi Beta Kappa, 1949, West Virginia University.

Alpha Omega Alpha, 1953, Indiana University.

Who's Who in the West, Vol. 10, Chicago.

Dictionary of International Biography, 1967, 4th Edition, London.

Teaching Positions and Appointments

Director of Medical Education, St. Mary's Long Beach Hospital, December, 1961-1964.

Clinical Instructor in Medicine, U.C.L.A. Medical School, 1962-1965.

Director, Lipid Research Foundation, 1969 to present.

Assistant Clinical Professor of Medicine, University of California, Irvine, College of Medicine, 1971.

Consultant for National Heart and Lung Institute, Special Programs Branch, September 21-21, 1972.

Subject Matter Expert, Health Learning Systems, Inc., Bloomfield, New Jersey, February 22, 1973.

Member of the Board of Visitors of the University of Minnesota, Study of Partial Ileal Bypass in the Treatment of the Hyperlipidemic States, June, 1973.

Medical Advisor to Administrative Law Judges, Bureau of Hearings and Appeals, Social Security Administration, Department of Health, Education and Welfare, October 9, 1973.

Chief, Department of Internal Medicine, Long Beach Community Hospital, 1974.

Professional Societies

Zumbro County Medical Association, 1960-1961.

Minnesota State Medical Association, 1960-1961.

American Association for the Advancement of Science, 1960 1961.

American Medical Association, 1960.

Los Angeles County Medical Association, 1962. California Medical Association, 1962.

Society of Nuclear Medicine, June 14, 1961 to 1964.

Alumni Association of the Mayo Foundation for Medical

Education and Research, October, 1962 to present.

Clinical Society, Diabetes Association of Southern California, 1963.

World Medical Association, 1963 to 1964.

American Diabetes Association, April 1, 1963.

Associate Fellow, American College of Cardiology, 1963. present.

Member, Board of Directors, Long Beach Heart Association, 1963.

Member, Long Beach Heart Association, 1963.

Member, American Heart Association, 1963.

Member, American Federation for Clinical Research, 1963.

Member, Long Beach Society of Internal Medicine, 1963.

Member, Long Beach Society of Internal Medicine, 1963.

Member, Order of St. Luke the Physician, 1963.

Fellow, American College of Angiology, March, 1964.

Fellow, American College of Physicians, April, 1966.

Long Beach Heart Association, Board of Directors, second appointment, 1970.

Long Beach Heart Association, Executive Committee, 1970. Affiliate of the Royal Society of Medicine, 1 Wimpole Street, London, April 3, 1973.

A Partial List of Publications by Dr. Casdorph

Ph.D. Thesis: "Studies of Cholesterol Metabolism: Relationships of the Body Cholesterol Pool Size, Cholesterol Turnover, and Hepatic Synthetic Rate of Cholesterol to the concentration of Plasma Cholesterol in the Dog." University of Minnesota, 1961

"The Education of the Diabetic." May 1963, *Newsletter*, Long Beach Lay Society of the Diabetes Association of Southern California.

"Hospital Experience with Cardiac Resuscitation." *California Medicine.* April 1964. Vol. 100: 248.

"Acute Uric Acid Nephropathy in Leukemia." *California Medicine.* 101:481-484, December 1964.

"Fats in the Diet." Symposium on Lipids, Atherosclerosis and Coronary Artery Disease. *Geriatrics.* Vol. 20:168-171, March 1965.

"Newer Concepts in Coronary Heart Disease." *Medical Times.* Vol. 92:1029, October 1964.

"Studies of Atrial Fibrillation in a Hospital Population Age, Sex, Associated Cardiac

Disease, Mode of Therapy and Complications." *Medical Times.* Vol. 93:293, March 1965.

"Acute Uric Acid Nephropathy in Leukemia," (Abstract) *Urology Digest.* Vol. 4:52, September, 1965.

"Treatment of Angina Pectoris." *Clinical Medicine.* Vol. 74: 1, January 1967.

"Cholestyranine, Therapy of Hypercholesteremia," *Progress in Biochemical Pharmacology,* Vol. 11. By Karger, in Basel.

"The Biologic Consequences of Hypercholesterenia in Man and its Treatment," *Angiology.* Vol. 18, No. 2, February 1967.

"Treatment of Hypercholesterenia," *JAMA.* Vol. 200:7, May 15, 1967.

"Treatment of Hypercholesteremia with Cliolestyramine, a Bile Acid Sequestering Resin," *Vascular Disease.* Vol. 4:305-308, October 1967.

"Hyperlipoproteinemia, " *JAMA.* Vol. 207:15 1, January 6, 1969.

"Safe Uses of Cholestyramine," *Annals of Internal Medicine.*, Vol. 72:759-760, May, 1970.

"Hypercholesteremia: Scourge of Western Civilization," *Medical Counterpoint.* Vol. 2 No. 11:12-22, November 1970.

"Diet and Drugs Successfully Treat Hyperlipidemia,"*Modern Medicine.* p. 8 2, May 3, 197 1.

"Management of Excess Serum Lipid," *The New England Journal of Medicine.* Vol. 284:1103, May 13, 1971.

"Cholestyramine Said to Reduce Serum Cholesterol, All Types," *Medical Tribune and Medical News.* Vol. 12:4, June. 16, 1971.

'The Aggressive Therapy of Type 11 Hyperlipidemia, (Familial Hypercholesteremia)," *Medical Tribune.* No. 45, Austrian edition, p. 30, 197 1.

Ed., *Treatment of the Hyperlipidemia States,* Springfield: Charles C. Thomas, 197 1.

"Normal Limits For Serum Cholesterols," *LANCET. Vol.* 1:1076, No. 759, May 13, 1972.

"What You Eat Might Lead to Heart Disease," *Memorial Mercury.* Vol. 13, p. 30-31, summer 1972, Long Beach Memorial Hospital publication.

With Connor, W.E., "Nutrition for Endurance Competition," *JAMA.* Vol. 222 No. 8, November 20, 1972.

"Familial Low Serum Cholesterol Levels in Obese Individuals, Questions and Answers," JAMA. January 27, 1975 Vol. 23 1, No. 4, p. 418.

"The Single Dose Method of Administering Cholestyramine." *Angiology.* Vol. 26, No. 2, October, 1975.

"Cholestyramine and Ion Exchange Resins," in *Lipid Pharmacology,* Paoletti, R. and Glueck, C.J. (editors). New York: Academic Press, 1976.